Praise for Dick Richards's *Artful Work* . . .
Winner of the Benjamin Franklin Award for Best Business Book of 1996

"In the tradition of Jim Autry, Max DePree, and other apostles of artful work, Dick Richards explores the processes and responsibilities of bringing spirit, soul, self, and art into the daily grind."

—BookPage

"Dick Richards offers challenging insights on how to exercise artful leadership, create a centered organization, see all work as spiritual work."

—Working from the Heart

"Richards reminds us, with charm and warmth, that, to the degree that we are whole persons, we are all also artists."

—Peter Koestenbaum, author of *The Heart of Business*

"Elegant . . . Richards looks to the world of art for inspiration about the nature of work . . . a book that will resonate for those who are already open to its holistic language and message. Those readers who aren't should read it anyway—maybe it will crack that deadened, mechanical vision of work that slipped in with the Industrial Age."

—Quality Digest

Continued . . .

"Wouldn't it be great if we could stop separating 'work' from 'life' and find a way to make it a more fulfilling part of our lives? Richards introduces a method for returning passion and commitment to the workplace . . . an innovative approach to a popular theme."

—*NAPRA Review*

"Compact, provocative, and inspirational . . . Mr. Richards gently escorts the reader into the new realm of work where artistry is once again united with industry."

—*Industry Week*

"A thought-provoking case for rethinking our view of work . . . inspirational, as well as practical."

—*Ethical Management*

"Lively reflections on how to derive joy and meaning from the workplace."

—*The Bookwatch*

"Artfully written."

—*Cincinnati Post*

Setting Your Genius Free

How to Discover

Your Spirit and Calling

DICK RICHARDS

Berkley Books, New York

This book is an original publication of The Berkley Publishing Group.

SETTING YOUR GENIUS FREE

A Berkley Book / published by arrangement with
the author

PRINTING HISTORY
Berkley trade paperback edition / March 1998

The Penguin Putnam Inc. World Wide Web site address is
http://www.penguinputnam.com

ISBN: 0-425-16165-X

BERKLEY®
Berkley Books are published by The Berkley Publishing Group,
a member of Penguin Putnam Inc.,
200 Madison Avenue, New York, New York 10016.
BERKLEY and the ''B'' design
are trademarks belonging to Berkley Publishing Corporation.

PRINTED IN THE UNITED STATES OF AMERICA

10 9 8 7 6 5 4 3 2 1

To the angels at Id-Dar tal-Provvidenza

Contents

Acknowledgments

Thank you.

Thank you, Calvin Germain and Marvin Israelow, for planting the seeds for this book.

Thank you, John Willig, Kathryn Hall, Karen Thomas, Natalee Rosenstein, and Steve Piersanti, for nudging my literary career along its sometimes ambiguous path.

Thank you, Lewis Portelli, Sylvia Ear, Anne Marie Morales, Lino Cuschierri, Achille Mizzi, and Grazio Falzone, for helping me appreciate the life of Monsignor Mikiel Azzopardi, and for helping me get the details right.

Thank you, Michelle Franey, George Davis, Cheryl Highwarden, Karen Schenk, Lora Whaley, Nancy Dawson, Beryl Byles,

Almut Klupp, Karen Adie, Paul Spearman, Ellen Foster, Scooter, Rob Henderson, Dee Conti, Dave Schmiege, and every single other person who has shared his or her genius and mission with me. I do not have a complete list, and I know it would be very long.

Thank you, Patti Schroeder, for being a spectacular sister and cohort in the crime of writing.

Thank you, Susan Smyth, for listening when I feel useless, helping me to make this and other parts of my life work, being kind, and for more things than I could possibly mention here.

Thank you all.

Introduction

This book is a celebration of what is good and right and true about each one of us. It is for the best part of yourself, your unique spirit.

Two fortunate events, both occurring nearly ten years ago, gave birth to this book. The first event took place in a small village on the southern coast of England, where I was leading a workshop for a large company, in partnership with my friend and sometimes colleague, Calvin Germain. Calvin, in his work as a coach to corporate leaders, used a concept that he called "Core Process," and which I have since come to know as "genius."

During our sojourn on the British coast, Calvin introduced me to techniques he used for helping his clients understand their Core Process, and he led me through the engaging—and sometimes frustrating—methods of discovering my own Core Process, my genius.

Those of us who work at guiding the development of others are always on the lookout for new ideas and techniques. I had a grab bag of them when Calvin said, "Here is something new and useful." But this concept of Core Process and the initial techniques I learned from Calvin seemed somehow more profound and powerful than anything I had ever encountered.

The second event occurred in New Jersey about a year after my meeting with Calvin. Another friend and sometimes colleague, Marvin Israelow, who worked for a large corporation, hired me as a consultant to develop a new training program for his company. The company was experiencing the beginnings of what we now call downsizing. It was an organization in which, historically, managers directed the careers of their subordinates. That was no longer entirely possible, as every manager's span of control was increasing rapidly. The company wanted to enable its people to manage their own careers more effectively, and this training program was one vehicle to achieve that end.

Designing a training program requires developing a conceptual model, a kind of road map or framework, that helps the designers, trainers, and participants understand what to include in the program, what to exclude, and how to create a sequence of events and concepts that lead to some desired outcome.

I decided that the concepts and methods I had learned from

Calvin were the perfect tools as a beginning point to help people take increased responsibility for their work lives and careers. I created a training program that included Core Process as a centerpiece, along with discussion of related issues such as commitment and personal mission.

This book loosely follows the structure of that workshop, and you will find a version of the conceptual model for the training program in chapter 8.

The program is still in existence as I write this, ten years later. Research about its effectiveness has led the company to continue to offer it for the benefit of its employees.

During the time between these two events and now, my understanding of Core Process has deepened, along with my own spiritual sensibilities. That is why I now call the extraordinary phenomenon that Calvin introduced to me "genius" rather than Core Process.

I have also found many other uses for the concept of genius. Friends, associates, and the executives I coach find it valuable, especially during times of transition in their work and careers. It helps them find direction. When teams that I consult with learn of each team member's genius, they discover a new appreciation for what each person contributes to their effort together. When a group of executives is forming a vision for their organization, understanding one another's genius is a valuable aid. They learn that, when the vision they create is connected in some way to each person's genius, they are more likely to succeed at communicating it to others and committing their energy to its realization.

Thus, the concept of genius and the techniques for finding your genius that this book contains have become the foundation of training in diverse areas such as leadership, career self-reliance, teamwork, and creativity.

As a result of these experiences, I now consider the concept of genius even more profound and powerful than when Calvin generously taught it to me. I have also developed other techniques for discovering genius, as well as a deeper understanding and appreciation for the power of the genius in each of us.

There is a mighty spirit infusing your activity and hovering protectively around you. That spirit is your genius. This book is your guide to discovering and nurturing it, detecting your purpose, exploring your commitments, and living a fulfilled life.

Setting Your Genius Free

How to Discover

Your Spirit and Calling

1

Your Genius

The forms of all things are derived from their
genius.
—WILLIAM BLAKE

You have a unique and special gift to give to the universe. My shorthand way of referring to your gift is to call it your genius.

The idea that we each have a genius may seem surprising or quite foreign, yet it is not a new idea but an ancient one that has become impoverished in our society. We tend to think of genius as a mental capacity, a number on an IQ test. The idea is much more fertile than that, and it has been alive in many cultures in many ages. For example, ancient Greeks and Romans believed genius was a spirit born at the same time as the person to whom it was attached. They believed the genius was carried by a person throughout that person's life and was a source of both direction and protection: a guiding star and guardian angel all wrapped in one package. Ancient Romans celebrated birthdays as the birth of a genius, not of a person.

Today, we are more likely to agonize over our apparent shortcomings and failures than to celebrate something unique and valuable about ourselves. In the time we take for self-reflection we are usually busy asking questions about what is wrong with us. Why can't I be more myself? Who am I, anyway? How did my family contribute to my dysfunction? What is my core addiction? How can I fix myself? Why can't I commit to a relationship? Why can't I find satisfying work?

Choose now to celebrate your value more often than you concern yourself with your shortcomings. Although it may be fruitful to shine the light of awareness on your problems and flaws, it is equally fruitful to bring your unique gifts out of the darkness. Your genius is one of those gifts.

This book will guide you to discover your genius and learn how to nurture it. Make no mistake: you have a genius. Your genius is your natural power. It holds the potential to create joy and success or frustration and failure when used without awareness and choice. Like any power, you will use it best if you understand it well.

In these pages you will find tools to help you discover your genius and create the situations in which your genius can flourish.

Give yourself the gift of believing that you have a genius. To my knowledge and by my imprecise calculations, about a thousand people in North America, South America, and Europe have attended workshops intended to help them discover their genius. They chose to give themselves that gift. Their experience has been that understanding their genius is both engaging and worthwhile.

This book also contains stories of people who have discovered their genius and what that discovery has meant to them. Here is one of those stories.

Francine: Engaging the Heart

Francine and I are feasting on fajitas—hers chicken, mine shrimp—on the sun-washed flagstone patio of a Mexican restaurant overlooking the Ohio River. We have been friends for many years and are as comfortable with sharing the details of our lives and thoughts as we are with the silence that sometimes punctuates our conversation.

Francine is a psychologist who works for a large corporation. Her job involves helping the company's managers develop themselves, their people, and the work environment. In the culture of this company, intellect and logic reign, hunches are suspect, and any display of emotion is grounds for a negative performance rating.

Francine tells me about a presentation she had attended on the previous day. The presenter showed a chart containing columns of figures to the audience. Several people immediately began tapping away at their calculators, checking the addition in the chart. "They were more interested in whether the addition was correct than in what the numbers meant," she says, "and they love to catch mistakes. They love to get one up on another person."

We talk about her genius, the gift she has to offer the universe, the gift that seems unwelcome in her present job. She describes her genius like this:

> I have to get right down to what matters, to the heart of things and to the hearts of the people I work with. When I do that, the sense is that words are somehow inadequate. Even in talking about my genius I sense that words don't work. When my heart is engaged, I know that something is good and right and has to be done. This is not an intellectual knowing nor is it a feeling exactly. It is a deep inner knowledge.
>
> I had to learn the logical stuff, and I am good at it. I know I am smart; I have all the degrees to prove it. However, I can't exist in that rational, logical framework all the time. There is more to life than being intellectually adept.

Francine calls her genius Engaging the Heart. In the next few chapters of this book, you will find a name for your genius.

It is hard to imagine an organizational climate more antithetical to Francine's genius; she is all heart and affirmation, while the people around her are all intellect and criticism. Her experience as an employee of the company is frustrating to her. She believes that she is not able to "get down to what really matters" with most of the people around her. Often, what really matters cannot be proven intellectually or with numbers.

Plaintively, she asks, "How do you measure the human spirit? How do you measure what is in the human heart? It certainly can't be done with a calculator."

This experience is frustrating for Francine because most of the people around her simply cannot see or do not value what she has to offer. They do not appreciate her gift. She is a rose attempting to bloom in a desert. She tells me, "This is not a good use of my life."

The situation has serious consequences for Francine. She says, "I feel angry at myself. When I first went into that situation, I was not fully aware of what I was in for. I kept thinking I should do something better, but I didn't know what to do. I would get irritated with myself, then mad at everybody else. I had a great deal of anger that was deadly to express in that climate. I beat myself up a lot."

Francine tells me she is leaving the company. Until now she was not certain why she had to leave; she only knew it was for the best. As she comes to a more complete understanding of her genius, the reasons for her leaving become more clear.

She says, "I am now searching for something that engages my heart, and I want to work with people who are doing the same."

Francine's genius was thwarted by the long-standing culture

of the company, the people around her who perpetuated that culture, and perhaps by her lack of skill in communicating what she was all about and what she had to offer. She believes that the situation was poisonous to her.

How to Use This Book

This book contains many stories similar to Francine's. These are stories of people who chose to leave a situation that was poisonous to their genius: a marriage, a job, a circle of friends. When you uncover and name your genius you also may recognize that your life situation requires change. Such a recognition will probably not be new to you. More likely, naming your genius will give you a way of understanding something you have known or sensed for some time: the need for change.

It is also possible that you will recognize why your current situation works well for you, if it does. You might also discover that minor changes, less dramatic changes than Francine's, will make an enormous difference to you.

When you understand the workings of your genius as well as Francine now does, you will be better able to avoid those situations that are poisonous to you. Better yet, you will also be able to actively seek those situations that are fulfilling and that enable you to be at your best. You will be better prepared to seek those situations that encourage a good use of your life.

The first five chapters of this book contain the tools for discovering your genius. Most of the tools involve writing and taking notes about yourself. Many people find it useful to keep a journal about their exploration to discover their genius, especially if they are working alone instead of in a group. Something small that you can carry around with you is best, or if you already carry a calendar or diary, you may want to devote pages to your genius. While using the tools, you will be filling your journal with information that contains clues about your genius.

Chapter 6 will help you pull all of the information together. You will give your genius a name, like Francine's Engaging the Heart. The name will allow you to hold onto your genius. The name is like a handle, permitting you to grasp the full meaning and complexity of your genius. Naming your genius correctly will give you the power to retain your awareness of it and claim it as yours.

Chapter 7 describes a group of people helping one another discover their individual geniuses, and offers guidelines for such groups. Working with a group, meeting to help one another, is an especially useful way to go about discovering your genius because other people often see things about us that we do not readily see. You will also find that, in such groups, people discover a deeper appreciation for one another.

Chapters 8 through 10 contain insights about how to follow your genius, nurture it, commit it to a mission, and gain the support you need to keep it alive.

The process of naming your genius also benefits from frequent reminders about the many facets of genius and the many different pathways the process might take. In workshops these reminders are taped on the wall as posters so that we all have them in front of us at all times. Having the posters in front of us helps immerse us in all of the details we need to keep in mind as we seek our individual geniuses. In this book some chapters end with "posters" that summarize key points from that chapter or from previous chapters. I suggest that you at least glance at them as you come upon them, even though you have already read the sections of the book that explain them. I have placed the posters at the ends of chapters so that they do not intrude; if you find them to be merely repetitious and annoying rather than helpful, you can skip them.

In my belief system, genius is an elusive spirit. It is elusive not because of any characteristic of the spirit itself but because we have ignored it for so very long and are not used to thinking about it, much less celebrating its existence. Perhaps, like so many of us, it has become elusive because it fears rejection.

I hope you will discover your genius because of this book. I hope you will detect your mission as well and discover new commitments or rediscover forgotten ones. I hope you will use this book as a map to a great adventure to capture and nurture what is good and right about yourself.

Two suggestions: First, this book contains many tools to help you detect your genius and also to discover your mission. Some people feel overwhelmed by the number of tools. Use the tools that make the most sense to you right now. If they do not work for you, use others, even if they do not make sense. The process of naming your genius is complex and does not lend itself totally to a linear step-by-step approach. Use as many of the tools as you need until you feel certain about your name for your genius; then use a few more to verify the name. Many people do not need to use all of the tools before a name for their genius seems obvious to them. Some geniuses are elusive critters, however.

Second, be gentle with yourself as you use the tools in this book. Be patient. Your genius is there, waiting for you. It may be shy because you have neglected it. Do not blame yourself for that. This book is intended as a celebration of what is good and right about you, and not a catalogue of your faults.

Core Principles

Understanding your genius is the first and necessary step to making good use of your life, to answering questions such as these:

What is the right work (or the wrong work) for me?

Why does the work I am doing seem fulfilling (or unfulfilling)?

What is the underlying source of my contentment (or frustration) with life?

Why do some relationships just seem to click (or not click)?

The answers to those questions lie within these four core principles for making good use of your life:

1. You have a genius, which is your unique and special gift to the universe in general, and to those around you in particular.
2. A good use of your life requires following your genius.
3. A good use of your life requires commitment to a mission.
4. Following your genius and committing to a mission are aided significantly by surrounding yourself with support.

These four principles are the foundation of the work you will do as you read further.

Old Bear

The children's book *Old Bear* tells of the rescue of a forgotten and aged teddy bear from a box in the attic by four stuffed friends, Bramwell Brown (another teddy bear), Duck, Rabbit, and Little Bear.

Old Bear's friends employ various methods in several attempts to reach the attic and set him free. Each of the friends offers a scheme. They build a tower of blocks. It collapses. They stand on one another's shoulders but fail again. They bounce on the bed but cannot achieve the required height. They climb a tall plant but break it. Finally, they succeed using an elaborate method involving a windup airplane and handkerchief parachutes. Old Bear is set free.

The story is primarily about the power of friendship. It is also about methods to rescue our own lives by releasing something forgotten, something of value.

Each of us may have an Old Bear, a forgotten and valuable piece of ourselves, confined in a box in a metaphorical attic.

After the bed-bouncing method fails, Duck laments, "What are we going to do now? We'll never be able to rescue Old Bear and he'll be stuck up there getting lonelier and lonelier for ever and ever."

Bramwell Brown answers firmly, "We mustn't give up."

We each have our own favorite method to rescue our lives. Our favorite method might be something like Stephen Covey's *The Seven Habits of Highly Effective People*, Deepak Chopra's *Seven Spiritual Laws of Success*, affiliation with a formal religion, or a twelve-step program. Or, perhaps, we are seeking a *Celestine Prophecy* moment.

The four stuffed friends, however, knew that their success would rest on something far more fundamental than any method they might invent. Their success would rest on their love for one another and for Old Bear.

Our success at rescuing or enhancing our own lives by setting free something valuable and forgotten will also rest on something far more fundamental than any method. No matter how powerful the method may be—and the ones mentioned above are all powerful—it will ultimately rest on knowledge of your own genius. For example, in *The Seven Spiritual Laws of Success*, Chopra wrote, "You have a talent that is unique in its expression, so unique that there's no one else alive on this planet that has that talent, or that expression of that talent." Chopra advises all of us to discover that talent. The talent is your genius.

As you read this book and use the tools it contains, you will discover your genius and determine whether it is alive or lying dormant, like Old Bear trapped in a box in the attic, waiting to be set free. You will discover how to use the power of your genius wisely. You will examine how your genius influences your relationships, work, habits, how you think, and what you believe.

Some people are skeptical about the notion of a genius, thinking the idea sounds too grandiose or too far outside the realm of possibility. It is neither. Are you skeptical? If you are, that may be because your genius has something to do with raising questions or seeking certainty. If you can accept that possibility, you have already begun learning about your genius. Suspend your disbelief long enough to read further.

A Thought Experiment

Giving a name to your genius is a thought experiment. A thought experiment is a scientific tool used to analyze theories. Galileo used thought experiments to test his theories, and Einstein used them liberally in exploring relativity. Most physicists accept the validity of thought experiments as a tool for examining reality.

You do not need to be Galileo or Einstein to do a thought experiment. All you must do is imagine that certain things are happening or are true, then examine the consequences of what you have imagined. For instance, Einstein discovered that the velocity of light was constant by imagining a situation in which people were observing light from a moving train.

To name your genius you will need to imagine that these things are true:

You do have a genius. I can offer no scientific proof that you have a genius. I have only my experience and the experience of the many others who have found their genius. You will either prove or disprove to yourself that you have a genius. The only way I know for you to do that is to involve yourself in this thought experiment. In other words, keep reading and do the suggested exercises in later chapters. If you doubt that you have a genius, try suspending your doubt and enter into the exercises in the next few chapters.

You have only one genius. At some point in the thought experiment, you may come to believe that you have two or more geniuses. The conditions of the experiment are that you have only one. I insist on this condition in order to force you to think more deeply about yourself. When people conclude they have more than one genius it is because they have not yet found their true genius. For example, Lyall, who calls his genius Surveying the Landscape, at first came to two names for his genius. One was Walking the Landscape, the other Looking for Truth. Walking the Landscape described his tendency to seek new ideas, thoughts, and experiences. When he realized that his metaphorical walking was in search of truth or new ideas, and that the word "walking" was too passive a description of what he did, he combined the two names into Surveying the Landscape.

Your genius has been with you your entire life. Your genius is not a transient nor a temporary thing, but has always been with you. It is natural to your being. When you name your genius you will recognize that you engaged it even as a small child. It is with you always. Joyce, who calls her genius Digging Deeper, says, "My genius gets up in the morning before I do." Diana, whose genius is Taking Care, says, "I know that my genius has been with me always. I believe it is undeniably and unavoidably the energy of my soul."

Your genius is a gift you give yourself and others. Your genius is your special and specific gift to the earth. Since you are part of the earth, you give this gift to yourself as well.

Your genius is natural and spontaneous and a source of success. You engage your genius often but probably do not notice it. It comes so naturally to you that it seems unremarkable or obvious to you. Yet it creates joy and success for you when you use it in the right situation.

Your genius is a positive force. If you arrive at a statement of your genius that feels negative to you, it is not your genius. Your genius is a positive force, an expression of what is good and right about you. You may at times engage it inappropriately or for damaging ends, but your genius itself is positive. While there is no doubt that evil exists in the world, the evil is not a product of genius. The existence of an "evil genius," a brilliant but destructive force, results from turning what is a positive force to destructive ends.

Your name for your genius may be literal or metaphorical, but it should contain only one verb and one noun. The verb should be progressive, that is, ending in the suffix -ing. This is to indicate that the action expressed by the verb is in progress. Your genius is working all of the time. When you give your genius a literal name you will use only one verb and one noun. The examples below describe people who have chosen a literal name for their genius. Their stories inhabit this book. As you read this list and the one below it, avoid the temptation to say, "This name fits me, too." Go through the process of finding your own name for your genius. The process is one of discovery rather than selection from a list. I estimate that I have guided about a thousand people through the process of finding their genius, and I cannot recall having heard the same name twice. Your genius is your unique gift, and I encourage you to discover your unique name for it. If one of the names below does resonate for you, treat that as a clue to your genius rather than the final word. Again, these are examples of literal names.

Francine's genius is Engaging the Heart.
Joyce's genius is Digging Deeper.

Martin's genius is Pursuing Understanding.

Mike's genius is Discovering Deeper Connections.

Diana's genius is Taking Care.

Melissa's genius is Overcoming Obstacles.

Dave's genius is Straightening Up.

Carmen's genius is Finding the Positive.

Marcel's genius is Considering Alternatives.

Mandy's genius is Making It Work.

Anne's genius is Feeling Deeply.

When you give your genius a metaphorical name, you will also use one verb and one noun, but the name may be longer than two words and will represent a metaphor. Examples are:

Frank's genius is Searching for Clues.

Sam's genius is Generating Warmth.

Myra's genius is Getting to the Bottom.

Steve's genius is Opening Doors.

Dan's genius is Charting the Course.

Jose's genius is Setting the Stage.

June's genius is Building Platforms.

Lyall's genius is Surveying the Landscape.

Andrea's genius is Making It Safe.

Marie's genius is Exploring Pathways.

Caroline's genius is Polishing Gems.

Van's genius is Building the Beyond.

Marianne's genius is Preparing the Way.

Your genius is not what you wish it would be, it is what it is. Be certain that the name you choose truly describes your genius and not what you think it should be or what you think might sound good to others. In genius workshops sponsored by corporations, people often name their genius something like Playing on a Team or Taking Risks. These names often arise when the company sponsoring the workshop is also trying to encourage team play and risk taking. You must look underneath these events to find your genius. For example, underneath Playing on a Team might be something like Making Connections or Building Energy.

If these conditions sound restrictive, they are. They are purposefully restrictive in order to give definition to the idea of genius. Uncovering and naming your genius is a creative process that will benefit from these restrictions.

Peeling the Onion

Naming your genius is like peeling an onion. You will peel away the outer layers. Those layers represent your behavior, what you say or do, as well as your talents or skills. You have developed the talents and skills you most enjoy because they allowed your genius to express itself. Your interests, creations, and accomplishments are also expressions of your genius.

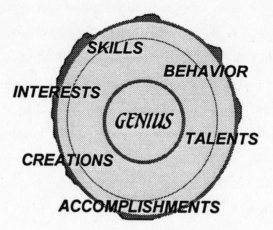

For example, I call my genius Creating Clarity. I have developed skill at communication, writing, photography, and teaching because they allow me to create clarity. Genius itself lies beneath those skills and talents, nearer to the center of the onion.

I named my genius ten years ago. I took me several months to arrive at a satisfactory name. Because of this book, it should not take you nearly so long.

Naming my genius helped me see my work and life more clearly. Creating Clarity is about understanding the world. It is about discovering ways of grasping complex ideas and phenomena. For example, in my work as a consultant to organizations and to individuals concerned with their own growth, I develop theoretical models to explain such things as customer service, career management, organizational purpose, self-responsibility, leadership, teamwork, and empowerment. I develop these models so that I can understand the phenomena that are important to my clients. I also find that my models are useful to others in planning processes and programs to deal with those issues. My skill at building models is near the skin of the onion; it is on the surface and is not my genius, which lies deeper.

I also love teaching because it helps me come to new awareness—greater clarity—about whatever subject I am teaching. I have taught mathematics, psychology, career management, organization change, management theory, team development, and customer service. I most enjoy teaching about something when I feel a need for greater clarity about it. Teaching, like creating conceptual models, is also a skill, nearer the outer surface of the onion.

Naming my genius also helped me with other kinds of work issues. For example, writing used to be torturous for me. I learned, as many of us have, "Write about what you know about." That injunction does not work for me. It sounds paradoxical, but I need to write about what I do not know about. Writing is a process of discovery for me; it is one way of Creating Clarity about something I am unclear about. When I am clear about something, I lose interest in writing about it, and the process is painful. In order to write this book, I have to approach it with the attitude that I am writing primarily to discover new facets of genius.

My genius is also at work in my hobbies. I am an amateur carpenter. I built a deck on my house and finished a hot-tub room with tongue-and-groove cedar. I do not plan to do either of those projects again. I am clear about how to do them and have no wish to repeat those experiences, even though they were pleasurable.

I am also an amateur photographer who tries to create clear images that provoke questions. One of my favorites among my photographs shows two joggers, a man and a woman, resting on the steps of a church in Key West. Dressed in a black T-shirt and shorts, the dark-haired man sits leaning forward, elbows on his knees, chin resting in his hands, covered in the shadows of a tree. She, on the other hand, is in full sunlight. Her jogging suit is white; her hair blond. She leans back, legs stretched out in front of her. His eyes are downcast, but she looks at him through the wrought iron bars of the railing that separates them. In short, the two people in this photograph are contrasts of light and shadow, open and closed. The railing between them suggests a barrier.

When others look at this image, they react in much the same way I did when I first saw it: "What is going on here?" Soon the picture becomes clear, although different people come to different conclusions about what is happening in the scene. Some conclude that the two people are angry at one another. Others believe he is ignoring her, while she is trying to attract his attention. Others merely see two people resting.

This photograph evokes in me and in others what my genius

is about: looking at something familiar but not well understood, and coming to some clarity about it. Many of my best photographs are like that.

My carpentry and photography are also near the surface of the onion. They are skills I have developed in part because they give expression to my genius.

Can you see the similarities between developing a theoretical model to explain customer service, teaching a variety of subjects, writing about things I don't quite understand, building a deck mostly for the pleasure of building a deck, and taking photographs that force the viewer to ask and answer the question, "What is going on here?" To me, all of those enterprises are about the same thing: creating clarity.

I see my genius at work in my relationships as well. My friends tell me that they are likely to turn to me when they feel confused about something in their lives. It is not that I have the answers, but I am good at the processes that help them produce their own answers: listening, coaching, counseling, synthesizing information, coming to a succinct conclusion. These skills are all strategies for gaining clarity that I learned and practiced in order to create clarity for myself. They also help me create clarity for others.

I hope you will see, by reading about my experience with my genius, that having a name for my genius has many benefits. It allows me to explain some of my most joyful and productive moments, thus giving me a greater chance of repeating them. It explains much of my frustration, allowing me to avoid frustration at best or understand it at least. Having a name for my genius also allows me to focus my attempts to make a difference in the world and in the lives of others. This book is one result of that focus.

Having a name for my genius also helps me understand why I am sometimes effective and sometimes not and why I enjoy certain activities and do not enjoy others. It helps me decide which projects I am most likely to feel good about and where I am most likely to succeed.

It also helps explain why relationships are satisfying or troublesome. Frank, whose genius is Searching for Clues, says, "Knowing my genius explains to me why some relationships just seem to click and why others, even though the other person and I might be speaking the same language, don't click. In the past, when a relationship didn't click, I used to agonize over it. Was there something wrong with me? With the other person? Now I often see exactly why it doesn't click. Sometimes I know what to do about that. Mostly, what is different is that I feel less inclined to change myself or wish the other person would change."

When you name your genius you will see that it is active in all of the important domains of your life: relationships, work, hobbies, spiritual beliefs, and family life. You will also have a potent tool to help make the important choices and decisions within those domains.

For example, Sam, who calls his genius Generating Warmth,

says about his work, "I was once in a job at which I was a complete failure. For years I thought that was because there was something wrong with me. When I understood my genius I could see that it was, quite simply, the wrong job for me. It didn't engage what is special about me. I was the proverbial square peg in a round hole."

The activities I engage in and described above are the outer layer of the onion I had to peel in order to find my genius beneath them. When you have peeled away all of the outer layers to find the core—your own genius—you will experience an Aha! The Aha!, like the onion, might even bring tears to your eyes, the kind of tears you might experience while greeting an old and treasured friend who you have not seen for a long time.

Some people are able to name their genius immediately after learning about the concept, but this is very rare. Even if you think you have the right name now, do the exercises in the following chapters; you may discover that you need to peel the onion further. Most people need to do all of the exercises and even then do not have a name that satisfies them. Some people arrive at a name, only to realize weeks or months later that it is not right. This is the process of peeling the onion, and there is no shortcut. However, along the way you will discover fascinating things about yourself, and I am certain you will find that the end point—having a name for your genius—is worth the effort.

Set your genius free. Retrieve it from the attic. Keep on creating and adopting whatever methods work for you as you improve your life, but understand that the success of those methods rests on something more fundamental: knowledge of your own unique genius.

Do not allow your genius to "be stuck up there getting lonelier and lonelier for ever and ever."

Detective Work

Naming your genius will take some detective work. The answer is there, somewhere. You have to find it.

There are three methods of detective work. I call them the Columbo method, the Holmes method, and the Millhone method, each named after a widely known detective.

Columbo, of television fame, trusted and used his intuitive powers to solve crimes. Peter Falk, as Columbo, stood before a suspect or witness, rumpled trench coat billowing around him, unlit cigar in hand, gently seeking the information he wanted. When finished, he turned as if to leave, only to turn back again, scratching his head with the hand that held the cigar in a way that always made me glad that it was unlit.

"I just have one more thing. Could you answer one more question? It's probably nothing, but . . ."

Sherlock Holmes, on the other hand, was all observation, logic, and deduction. At the conclusion of one adventure, he tells his assistant, Watson,

An inspection of his chair showed me that he had been in the habit of standing on it, which of course would be necessary in order that he should reach the ventilator. The sight of the safe, the saucer of milk, and the whipcord were enough to finally dispel any doubts which may have remained . . . Having once made up my mind, you know the steps which I took to put the matter to the proof.

Kinsey Millhone, the heroine of Sue Grafton's alphabetized novels, seems to stumble fearlessly onto answers rather than intuit or deduce them.

The key rattled in the lock and my head whipped up. Fear shot through me like a jolt of electricity and my heart started thudding so hard it made my whole neck pulse. My single advantage was that I knew about them before they knew about me.

This is detection by experience.

Intuition, deduction, and experience are all methods that will help you find a name for your genius. The tools at the end of some chapters of this book will help with your detection process. Some tools provide data, which is food for deduction. Others will tap your intuitive powers. Some will offer experiences, although not the life-and-death kind of experiences that visit Kinsey Millhone.

Most of us are more adept at one method than the others. In truth, all three detectives utilized all three means of detection. Try the tools that seem unnatural to you as well as the ones that seem comfortable.

The next chapter describes one tool: noticing. Learning what to notice will help you begin finding a name for your genius. Do not be concerned if you are not completely certain about what genius actually is. It will be defined more clearly in chapter 3.

2

Noticing

How can I be useful, of what service can I be?
There is something inside me, what can it be?
—VINCENT VAN GOGH

In 1926, physicists Werner Heisenberg and Neils Bohr spent many long nights in Copenhagen arguing and puzzling over newly born theories of quantum mechanics. In February 1927, Bohr decided to get away from it all to go skiing in Norway. Heisenberg was glad to be left behind where, he said, "I could think about these hopelessly complicated problems undisturbed."

In his writing about this period of solitude, Heisenberg described the obstacles before him as insurmountable. He wondered if he and Bohr had been asking the wrong questions. He tried to make connections between seemingly mutually exclusive facts.

He recalled something that Einstein had told him, "It is the theory which decides what we can observe." Heisenberg wrote:

27

I was immediately convinced that the key to the gate that had been closed for so long must be sought right here. I decided to go on a nocturnal walk through Faelle Park and to think further about the matter.

It was on this walk that Heisenberg formulated what is now called the uncertainty principle of quantum mechanics. It was a breakthrough that changed the world of physics.

Later, he wrote that his theory "established the much needed bridge."

We will never know how Heisenberg might have described his own genius. We can, however, make educated guesses by noticing his behavior and how he describes it. He is Overcoming Obstacles. He is Establishing Connections. He is Seeking the Key, and Establishing the Bridge.

The simplest thing you can do to name your genius is notice yourself in the same way we just noticed Heisenberg's process and how he described it.

In particular, notice what you do when you are not noticing what you do. Yes, it sounds paradoxical: *Notice what you do when you are not noticing what you do.*

Your genius comes spontaneously and easily; it is so natural to you that you probably do not notice it. So begin noticing!

Noticing what you do when you are not noticing what you do is a powerful way of generating information about your genius because it requires you to attend to information that you usually ignore. Attending to information that you usually ignore will often enable you to see things differently. For example, when I consult to organizations, I am often aware that many managers attend to only one kind of information: intellectual information formed of thoughts, ideas, and numbers. Usually, they ignore emotional information, even though it is often right in front of them. How people feel about their work and what happens in their workplace has an enormous impact on how they perform. Attending to emotional information would frequently force managers to manage very differently than they do because they would see things they do not normally see.

I do not know the ultimate source of the lines below, yet they have been a powerful reminder to me about the importance of noticing what I do not usually notice.

If I continue to take in data as I have always taken in data,
Then I will continue to think as I have always thought.
If I continue to think as I have always thought,
Then I will continue to believe as I have always believed.
If I continue to believe as I have always believed,
Then I will continue to act as I have always acted.
If I continue to act as I have always acted,
Then I will continue to get what I have always gotten.

These lines suggest that using different kinds of information than you normally use will open the door to change in your life.

The stories told in this book, about people who have gained knowledge of their geniuses, attest to the profound difference that knowledge can make. It does, however, require examining new data.

Naming your genius provides a way of seeing yourself differently than you normally do, creating a new belief about yourself. Because of that new belief, you may act differently. Because of this different action, you may get something other than you have always gotten. In order to set this chain of causality into motion you will have to attend to different information than you normally do. You may have to begin noticing things about yourself that you usually take for granted.

Dave: Straightening Up

Dave is a chemical engineer. When I met him he had been in a managerial job at a chemical company for two years. Bored with his job and concerned that his boredom was beginning to influence his performance, Dave arrived at a career development workshop eager to figure out what he might do next.

Naming genius was a central feature of that workshop, and for the first day and a half Dave sought his genius with much enthusiasm but little success. After the lunch break on the second day of the workshop, Dave returned to the meeting room. In the front of that room stood a flip chart stand holding a large pad of paper. The pad had been rolled up before being placed on the stand and did not lie flat. Also in the room was a large potted plant, knocked awry and standing crookedly.

Dave walked into the room, went to the flip chart and smoothed it with his hand, went to the plant and straightened it, arranged a few chairs, and sat down. I pointed out to him what he had done. He had not really noticed his behavior, as it just seemed natural for him to fix the flip chart, straighten the plant, and organize the chairs. He did not think much about it. He just did it.

This type of behavior is often a clue to genius; it is spontaneous, unplanned, and often carried out without awareness.

Dave then began making connections between his behavior with the chart, plant, and chairs, and other aspects of his life. He told us about his home workshop where he got as much enjoyment out of organizing his tools and supplies as anything else he did in it. He also talked about his first days at his current job, when he found the group that he manages in disarray. He talked about how he had cleaned up the mess he found there, and about how things were now running smoothly.

From this discussion Dave arrived at a name for his genius: Straightening Up. Straightening Up is what he had done with the flip chart, plant, and chairs. It is what he did in his home workshop, and what he did in the beginning in his job. Dave also realized what was wrong in his job at the moment: there was nothing more to straighten up, so he felt bored.

Naming his genius was an important milestone in Dave's career, as he realized that he was happiest and most successful in jobs where he had a lot of straightening up to do. He resolved to seek jobs and tasks that would allow him to be at his best.

I was the one who noticed Dave's behavior. Here is an example of a person who did her own noticing.

June: Building Platforms

During a similar workshop to the one Dave attended, June noticed that she took notes in a much more comprehensive and disciplined way than anyone else. She also noticed that it was she who suggested that the group create a list of names and phone numbers so people could call one another after the workshop. This behavior felt familiar to June. She connected it to two hobbies, sewing and gardening. June is not an avid seamstress, but she does enjoy buying patterns and has a drawer full of them. She expects that she will never use some of the patterns, but she feels comforted by their presence in her apartment. They are available whenever she feels the urge to sew. As a gardener, she enjoys planning and preparing the garden and planting the seeds far more than tending it and even more than harvesting it.

June works for a large corporation that is undergoing the turmoil familiar to many of today's companies. Although her training is as a systems analyst, she accepted a temporary assignment on a team the company formed to help it through its turbulent change process. The work of the team involved leading training programs and helping other teams become more effective. June loved this work and was considering a career change.

When June noticed herself taking notes and organizing a phone list, she began a long and thoughtful journey to name her genius. She arrived at the name Building Platforms. She takes copious notes because she wants to use them as a platform for her learning. She wants to have them to refer to. The phone list was, for June, a platform upon which to create a support network of people engaged in the work of naming their genius. Her drawer full of patterns was a platform that she could draw on whenever the urge to sew came upon her. As a gardener, she got the most pleasure out of preparing the platform for her garden, making the soil ready, and planting the seeds. And the reason June's new work was so exciting was that she saw herself as helping to create a platform for her company's future prosperity. She gives herself many platforms as gifts, and so wanted to provide others in the company with a platform as well.

Naming her genius helped June make an important career choice. When she realized how the work of being an organization change agent connected to her deepest sense of her mission in life, she made a commitment to pursue this new career path.

Making Connections

Noticing is crucial to naming your genius. However, as Dave's and June's experiences show, noticing, by itself, is not enough. What you do with what you notice is equally important.

Both Dave and June were able to connect what they noticed with other aspects of their lives. Dave connected his classroom behavior with his workshop and his job. June connected creating a phone list with her hobbies and her new work assignment. Your work and your hobbies contain important clues to your genius; especially your hobbies, because they may contain more of a sense of being your choice than does your work.

After you make the connections, ask yourself, "What is similar about all of these activities or behaviors?" And ask, "What is it about these skills or activities that I enjoy the most?" Also ask, "What gift am I giving myself or offering others?"

Noticing draws your attention to surface behavior and activities. Your genius is an undercurrent sweeping along beneath the surface. It can often be detected by making connections between your intentions in what appear to be different situations and circumstances.

Is Your Genius in Your Way?

At this point you may believe that you have the right name for your genius. If you do, try saying aloud, "My genius is _____ _____." See how it feels. Does it feel right, or is there some nagging doubt lurking about? Whatever happens, trust it. Although some people do discover their genius very quickly, most people go through two or three names before it feels just right. Do not worry about that. Accept the name you have for your genius now, if you have one, and continue with the next exercise. If it is right, it will still feel right as you go on. If it is not, you will get closer to the right name.

One warning: Sometimes the workings of a genius make it difficult to name the genius. For example, Marcel, whose genius is Considering Alternatives, had a difficult time settling on a name for his genius. As soon as he believed he had the right name he would immediately begin considering alternatives. When he noticed himself doing that, the correct name became obvious to him.

Myra, whose genius is Getting to the Bottom, had a similar difficulty. Each time she settled on a name she would seek one underneath it. She, too, noticed what she was doing.

Of course, there are also geniuses that make it easier to name your genius. Mike, for example, calls his genius Discovering Deeper Connections. He thoroughly enjoyed the process of making the connections that led him to name his genius and came to his name rather quickly. Again, the trick is to notice what you are doing as you try to name your genius.

Getting It Right

''How will I know when I've gotten it right?'' is the question many people ask at this point.

The answer is that when you have gotten it right, you will know it is right. I have watched many people name their genius. Almost always, when they have it right, they know it, and I can see that they know it. A look of recognition and pleasure spreads over their faces. It is as if they are looking in a mirror, seeing themselves clearly for the first time, and really liking what they see. Watch for that feeling. When you feel it, you will know you have gotten it right. I will have more to say about this in a later chapter.

What Your Genius Is Not

Your genius is not Helping Others or Doing Good. By definition, your genius is a gift you have to offer. The question is, "What is your special way of helping others or doing good?"

Although names such as Helping Others or Doing Good do not describe genius, your desire to choose them as names for it can be a valuable clue. For example, Anne first thought her genius was Helping Others. When challenged to peel the onion further, she realized that her true genius was Feeling Deeply, and because she feels things deeply, she empathizes easily with others and wants to help them. As a rule, words like "others" and "people" are not part of your genius. Remember that whatever gift you have is also a gift for yourself.

Aha!

Another lesson to be taken from the story of Heisenberg's famous walk in the park concerns the nature of the Aha! process. Heisenberg and his associates had been puzzling over their problem for months; studying it, reading about it, and talking with one another. We might say that they were trying to wrestle the problem to the ground. Then, Heisenberg let go, and the answer appeared.

Such letting go, walking away from a problem, is often necessary to the creative leap that produces the Aha! experience.

Experts in creativity explain this phenomenon as a product of the unconscious breaking through to the conscious. While you are consciously using the tools I have provided to help you find a name for your genius, your subconscious is also working at the same task. Letting go of your efforts, stopping the active conscious process of collecting data about your genius, may allow the subconscious to provide you with the name for your genius.

Mike arrived at a name for his genius while jogging. Melissa found hers in a dream. Steve was sitting lazily along a stream, fishing for trout.

As you use the tools, fill your conscious mind with data. Then let go for a while. The Aha! is your subconscious breaking through the chatter of your conscious mind. You cannot force this to happen. All you can do is divert yourself into some basically mindless activity like taking a walk or a bath or a nap.

Tools for Noticing

Use a day or two (or more) to notice, and to use the tools below.

The next chapter describes the many facets of genius. Its intent is to deepen your understanding of the concept of genius, not necessarily to help find a name for yours. In chapter 4 we will return to finding a name for your genius. So, you can use the tools below while reading the next chapter. Remember, it isn't necessary to use all of these tools. I suggest you read through them and choose those that appeal to you. If, after reading the first seven chapters, you have not arrived at a name for your genius, come back to the tools you skipped.

• NOTICING

What is the first thing you think about when you enter a room?

What is the first thing you do when you enter a room?

When you are in a group, what do you do that contributes to the group?

What do you add to conversations with others?

What do you enjoy doing when you are alone?

• ASKING "WHY?"

Ask yourself, "Why am I doing what I have noticed I do?" Ask in a nonjudgmental way, in a spirit of curiosity about yourself. Look at yourself with soft eyes, eyes that are uncritical, rather than hard eyes, which are critical and judgmental.

Do not allow the question, "Why am I doing what I have noticed I do?" to lead you into analysis of your past or condemnation of your motives. Just be curious. Remember that the purpose of all of these tools is to collect information and not to analyze or judge it.

If the question seems to lead you into judgment or criticism, try asking, "What am I trying to create or contribute?"

• YOUR GIFT

What is the gift you repeatedly give to others? For example, Dave, who calls his genius Straightening Up, rearranged the plant, flip chart, and chairs for the people who would soon follow him into the room. June, true to her genius of Building Platforms, created a mailing list of the people at the meeting she attended.

• CONNECTING

Examine your answers to the questions above and to your notes about what you notice about yourself. Are there any similarities? Your genius is an undercurrent sweeping along beneath the surface of your life. This undercurrent can often be detected by observing how, in many seemingly different situations, you are engaged in the same activity beneath the surface of your behavior.

Lyall, whose genius is Surveying the Landscape, reads copiously, travels extensively, and talks to many people. Books, the places he visits, and the people he meets are all his landscapes. When he reads, travels, and converses, he is seeking, as if through a surveyor's transit, for important markers.

• **WHAT YOU ENJOY**

List twenty things you most enjoy doing. Do not agonize over this list; write quickly. It does not matter if the list is perfect. When you have finished, look at the list, asking, "What is similar about these activities?"

• **IT'S NATURAL**

List activities or behavior that seem to come very naturally to you. Again, do not agonize over the list; write quickly. Do you see anything similar in the activities or behavior you have listed.

• **SKILLS**

List the skills you have developed or practiced during your life. For each skill, list answers to the question, "What does this skill accomplish?" Does any pattern emerge from these lists?

• **NOTICING THE PROCESS**

Your genius is active in your attempts to name it. Notice your process as you go about using these tools. This will be particularly helpful if you find yourself stuck or are generating many names with no sense of rightness about any of them. Remember the difficulty Marcel encountered because his genius, Generating Alternatives, led him to consider alternative after alternative.

• USING IMAGES

One of my favorite sculptures is Rodin's "The Thinker," and a small African statue of a person in deep contemplation sits on my desk. A small pewter statue of Merlin, with his crystal ball, owl, and magic wand, lives on the desk also. These two statues, both given to me as gifts, are representations of my genius, Creating Clarity. The friends who gave them to me know me well and appreciate my genius. They recognized me in these figures. Both friends said, "This reminded me of you," when they gave me the statues.

Notice what images attract you. In particular, notice images of people: photographs, paintings, drawings, sculpture. Can you identify with any of the people in the images? What are they doing? What do you think they are getting out of what they are doing? What are they doing that other people would appreciate? In what way do you identify with them?

Imagine yourself in the place of the people who attract you in such images. Write a brief account of what you are doing as that person. Search the words in your account for clues to your genius. What gift do you bring to the situation depicted in the image?

• CREATING IMAGES

Draw, paint, sculpt, crayon, or finger paint your genius. Put on some music and dance the way your genius dances. Pick up a musical instrument and play the way your genius plays. When you do these things, you may see your genius. If you do, you can give it a name.

• PROJECTION

If you have Tarot cards or some other method of divination, you can use them in a different way than you normally use them to gain clues to your genius. Instead of selecting one at random, select one that appeals to you. What does it tell you about your genius?

• JOHN LENNON'S GENIUS

Naming your genius and deciding for yourself exactly what this spirit is does not all have to be hard work. Enjoy it. One way to do that is to play with the idea of genius by trying to give a name to the genius of historical figures, just as I tried to do about Werner Heisenberg at the beginning of this chapter. What was John Lennon's genius? What historical figure do you have enough information about to make an educated guess about his or her genius?

Conditions of the Experiment

- You do have a genius.
- You have only one genius.
- Your genius has been with you your entire life.
- Your genius is a gift you give yourself and others.
- Your genius is natural and spontaneous and a source of success.
- Your genius is a positive force.
- Your name for your genius may be literal or metaphorical, but it should contain only one verb and one noun.
- Your genius is not what you wish it would be, it is what it is.

3

What Is Genius?

No man . . . can be a genius; but all men have a genius, to be served or disobeyed at their own peril.

—ANANDA COOMARASWAMY

My understanding of the concept of genius has changed over the years I have studied it. My first understanding of genius was rather mechanistic; I thought of it as a process occurring within me, part psychological and part physical. As my spiritual sensibility has increased and deepened, my understanding of genius has become more spiritual. This chapter explains all of the ways I have understood genius. They are not contradictory but complement one another, each definition adding new insights and depth of meaning.

Read all of the beliefs and decide which way of thinking about your genius makes the most sense to you right now. It does not matter where you begin, only that you begin. As you progress in the work of naming and learning to respect your genius, your way of thinking about it may develop new twists just as mine has.

Problems and Mysteries

As you read the varied beliefs about genius that follow, keep in mind that there is a difference between a problem and a mystery.

A problem lends itself to intellectual analysis and to quantification. Problems generate solutions. Mysteries, on the other hand, do not have solutions. They involve the questions to which there are no objective answers; no answers beyond the answers that we create out of belief and faith. Mysteries are meant to be explored. What is beautiful? What is God? What is the meaning of my life? Am I free, or is my life predetermined? What does it mean to be alone? These are mysteries because we have only the questions we ask and the answers we create and believe.

People differ in their explanations of mysteries, and everyone can be right because there is no ultimate right. Just as problems generate solutions, mysteries generate beliefs. Genius is a mystery. Is it this? Or that? No one knows for sure, although at different times and places people of different cultures have held beliefs about genius or something quite like it.

My wish is that the beliefs about genius described below will stir you to formulate your own beliefs about your genius.

Core Process

I first heard about genius from my friend and colleague, Calvin Germain, who called it "Core Process." Calvin described Core Process as the spontaneous and unique sequence of events that happens within you when you encounter information from the external world, then react to that data.

To understand the idea of Core Process, imagine yourself as a box. Inside the box there is some activity happening. Data comes into the box at one end. Something happens to the data within the box, and something comes out of the box at the other end. The thing that happens inside the box is the Core Process. For me, Core Process involves scanning the world for things I want to understand, then going about the process of understanding them. My shorthand way of saying that is Creating Clarity.

Although I now prefer to call it genius, I still find the notion of Core Process useful. It evokes the idea that genius resides at my core, at the very center of who I am. It also recognizes genius as an ongoing process rather than a result.

Natural Power

Although the idea of Core Process served me well during my first phases of learning about genius, the term seemed lacking in some way. During a workshop in which genius (I was still calling it Core Process at the time) was a central feature, a woman raised in the Hindu tradition said that the concept sounded very much like what she called Dharma. She described Dharma as the essential quality of a person.

In *The Seven Spiritual Laws of Success*, Deepak Chopra described his seventh law as The Law of Dharma. According to this law, each of us has a unique talent and unique way of expressing it. Chopra wrote,

> The Law of Dharma says that every human being has a unique talent. You have a talent that is unique in its expression, so unique that there is no one else alive on this planet that has that talent, or that expression of that talent. This means that there is one thing you can do, and one way of doing it, that is better than anyone else on this entire planet.

That talent, and your expression of it, is your genius.

Prior to learning about Dharma, I had not viewed the Core Process as essential, I had seen it only as something natural.

The distinction between "essential" and "natural" became important to me because in the term "essential," I experience an imperative that I do not experience in the term "natural." The difference is the difference between, "It is only natural that I do this," and, "It is essential that I do this!"

This distinction is expressed at the beginning of this chapter in a quote from Ananda Coomaraswamy, a linguist, philosopher, and art historian.

Although I have known about my genius for about fourteen years, there was a period of nearly four of those years during which I ignored it totally. This period began when some deep unconscious part of me recognized that my marriage was not working. As this was not my first marriage, I was eager to have it work—I did not want to "fail" again—but experienced a very confusing and painful lack of clarity about what was happening. For me, lack of clarity about something as important as a marriage is devastating. I also believed my wife contributed significantly to my confusion, and that it was hopeless to expect that to change. I remember vividly the moment, sitting on the stairway in our home, when I decided that I had to stop trying to Create Clarity about the situation. My sanity demanded it. I cannot say that I knew exactly what I was doing at the time. With the advantage of hindsight, I know that I was denying my genius because it was frustrated in my marriage and the frustration was becoming too painful.

I lived in that denial for about four years. My genius found expression in my work, and so I worked as I never had before and never will again. Toward the end of this period I worked on a project that called for me to teach once again about genius, and in doing so I rediscovered my own. Shortly thereafter my marriage ended.

I do not mean to suggest that denial or violation of my genius is the only reason my marriage failed. There are many lenses we might place on our perceptual camera as we view life. There are psychological lenses that help us understand such things as the effect of our family of origin or our own strengths and weaknesses. There are religious, political, and philosophical lenses, each providing a different view of reality. The more lenses we have, the more able we will be to deal with life's challenges and to create of ourselves the best people we can be. Knowing your genius is another lens in your repertoire, and it is one way of looking at what happened in my marriage.

I do mean to say that the situation of my marriage was toxic to my genius, and that made the marriage intolerable for me. In other words, I was unable to respect my genius in my marriage, so I had to end it.

During my four-year denial of my genius I also began a lifestyle that helped me maintain my denial. I traveled more than was healthy for me and frequently sedated myself with alcohol. I kept score on my life by how much money I made and how many frequent flier miles I accumulated. I stopped writing; writing is a highly personal act for me, and I simply could not get that close to myself nor spend the time alone with myself that writing requires. I did not see all of this at the time; that is the nature of denial. Since I rediscovered my genius, I have had to change those habits because they are not respectful of it. Respecting my genius has become a test of whether my life is healthy or not. I seek friends and activities that engage it, and I avoid people and situations that are toxic to it. As you know, I am writing again.

The work of respecting your own genius might lead you to find aspects of your life that require change. On a more optimistic note, you might discover why everything feels right to you now, and you will know more about how to maintain that feeling. I do not want to scare you off by implying that respecting your genius will be painful or will cause enormous disruption in your life. It may, and it may not. If it does, you will at least have a test for the changes you must make. The test is: Is this change respectful of my genius?

Genius Is Essential

During an afternoon of stimulating conversation, a new friend told me that he wanted to write a book. "I must do this," he said. "I am convinced this book is inside me and will destroy me if I don't let it out." He said this with a good deal of conviction and passion, and with a hint of desperation as well. Your genius is like my friend's book. It wants to be let out, released to serve the world. It is essential—essential to the world and to you.

After my encounter with the Indian woman, I began referring to "genius," although at the time I was not sure exactly what the term meant. It just felt right. I began reading about the concept of "genius" and the more I discovered about the concept the more I liked the term.

Can you sense in all of this my attempt to Create Clarity?

The dictionary definition of genius that fits most closely with the way I am using the word is, "A natural ability or capacity." That definition helped me understand my genius as a natural part of me in the sense that it comes naturally. My genius is always at the ready, seeking opportunities to manifest itself.

Another dictionary definition is, "strong inclination." I am strongly inclined toward my genius, as you are toward yours, although you may not be aware of the inclination until you name your genius. However, the dictionary definitions of genius fall short of the meaning I intend because it does not describe the actual quality of genius. It does not tell us, "What kind of ability is this?"

Genius in Classical Rome and Greece

One answer to that question lies in the mythology of ancient Rome and Greece. The Romans, as I mentioned at the beginning of chapter 1, thought of genius as a spirit born when a person was born, and it was attached to that person throughout his or her life. It played a role in all major events of the person's life: birth, marriage, death, and so forth. It was a power that generated hope and a wellspring of optimism. Its primary purpose was sustaining the life of the individual. The feminine form was called a juno.

This genius was both an interior force and a spirit guide: a guide to be followed, which dwelled not wholly within nor without the person.

In Greek mythology the genius was called a daimon. It was believed to be a semidivine being, or demigod, the offspring of a divine and human parent.

Plato wrote that at creation each soul goes before the three Fates, the goddesses of destiny. The first is Lachesis.

And she sent with each, as the guardian of his life and the fulfiller of his choice, the genius that he had chosen, and this divinity led the soul first to Clotho, under her hand and her turning of the spindle to ratify the destiny of his lot and choice; and after contact with her the genius again led the soul to the spinning of Atropos to make the web of its destiny irreversible, and then without a backward look it passed beneath the throne of Necessity.

Plato's genius leads the soul through the process that gives it a mortal reality. This genius is chosen by the soul as the guardian of the life it is about to begin.

When attached to a person, the daimon controlled his or her destiny. It also led each person into death. Plato wrote,

And so it is said that after death, the tutelary genius of each person, to whom he had been allotted in life, leads him to a place where the dead are gathered together, then they are judged and depart to the other world.

Plato also calls the genius "tutelary," suggesting that it is a guide or teacher. Socrates experienced his daimon as a divine presence within himself that would warn him if he was about to do something foolish.

In classical Greece these beings were viewed as beneficial, but in later times we have come to think of them as evil. The word "demon" derives from "daimon."

To summarize, the classical idea of genius was of a spirit that springs into being at your birth and attends you throughout your life as a source of sustenance, power, and guidance. It leads your soul into birth and death. It is not wholly inside you nor outside but exists in both realms.

This set of classical beliefs provides the framework in which we can think of genius as a gift from the soul. In *The Soul's Code*, James Hillman wrote, "You are born with a character; it is given; a gift, as the old stories say, from the guardians upon your birth." Hillman has also found evidence of genius in West Africa, Haiti, South America, and among native peoples in North America.

Robert Bly alludes to it in *The Sibling Society*, when he speaks of each person having a "spiritual twin."

At birth the two of you (you and your spiritual twin) separated, and perhaps you might not see your spiritual twin again in this life, although you would always long for her or him. In such a culture, the candles at the birthday party are lit for the twin, not for you. There is a hint of that in Russian birthday celebrations, in which a person shares a name-day with a saint; so one's birthdate is also a celebration for that saint. In American birthday parties, the little boy or girl thinks the cake and the candle are for them; there is no hint of any other being, to whom one might be grateful.

So there is a sense of longing when the genius is absent. And, as Coomaraswamy warned, peril.

In a letter to a friend, William Blake wrote,

I find more and more that my style of designing is a species by itself, and in this which I send you have been compelled by my genius or angel to follow where he led; if I were to act otherwise it would not fulfill the purpose for which alone I live. . . .

I find this view of genius as a combination guardian angel and spirit guide appealing because it emphasizes the notion that genius is a power that is always with me, providing inspiration, guidance, hope, and protection. I hear, in this notion of genius, echoes of a force that requires expression; a force that is not only natural but essential.

Combining the dictionary definition of ''genius'' as a natural ability with the classical idea that genius is a power, we can arrive at a synonym for genius: ''natural power.''

The Energy of the Soul

The idea of a soul is present in spiritual traditions in many forms. Most often, souls are believed to be entities or spirits that exist outside our dimensions of time and space, and they express themselves in the physical world through us. Souls do this because it is their way of evolving. They incarnate many times to express whatever they need to express in order to become more highly evolved. When a soul enters the physical realm it does so to heal itself. It brings with it the energy required to perform that healing. I call this energy your genius.

In his book, *The Seat of the Soul*, scientist and philosopher Gary Zukav describes the soul, saying, ''It is a positive, purposeful force at the core of your being.'' That is also a good description of genius.

Diana, who calls her genius Taking Care, says, ''This is how my soul has chosen to express itself in this lifetime. Knowing this is a big plus. I waste less energy. I focus on what is important in my life. I am more productive.''

Soul's purpose. Core Process. Natural power. All are useful ways of thinking about your genius. It is a natural ability, a strong inclination, a spirit, and a power. It is a process at your center and your reason for being. Hillman refers to is as an "acorn": ". . . each person bears a uniqueness that asks to be lived and that is already present before it can be lived."

Throughout the remainder of this book I will speak of genius in the sense that the ancient Greeks and Romans spoke of it; as your guardian angel and guiding star. However, it is not necessary for you to accept my spiritual beliefs in order to benefit from naming and respecting your genius. My initial discoveries about my genius did not require a spiritual aspect to be meaningful, nor will yours. However, as my spiritual sense of genius has grown, so has my willingness to do the things required of me to place my genius closer to the center of my life. As you read further you will discover many choices you might make to increase the centrality of your genius in your life. I believe that your willingness to make those choices will be in proportion to your willingness to view your genius from a spiritual perspective.

Nature or Nurture

Invariably, when I speak to other people about genius, this question arises: Is genius inborn and the product of genetics, or is it learned? Invariably, my answer is: I don't know.

Furthermore, if we think of genius in the classical sense, or as the energy of the soul, the question becomes moot. People who work with genius develop their own sets of beliefs about what it really is. Here are two examples.

Andrea works as an outdoor education specialist. She leads training programs involving activities such as rock climbing and ropes courses. She calls her genius Making It Safe. Watching her show people how to climb and use the required safety equipment is a clear demonstration of a genius in action.

Andrea's parents died soon after her birth. She spent the first year of her life in a succession of foster care situations. She was then adopted by the people she would come to think of as parents. As an adult, Andrea carried a vague memory of being "drowned in my crib." She mentioned it to her adoptive mother who explained its meaning.

When Andrea was eighteen months old, her adoptive mother was having problems with her back and was under orders not to lift anything. One day Andrea was crying inconsolably and her mother, heartbroken but unable to lift her, called Andrea's former social worker for help. The social worker, upon hearing Andrea's cries, doused her with a large glass of water.

Andrea says, "I could not have felt very safe as an infant, what with being shunted from one foster situation to another and the behavior of my social worker." Andrea believes that she learned her genius as a result of those experiences.

Marianne's belief about her genius is quite different. At the age of forty-three, she was in an automobile accident in which the two friends riding with her were killed. She suffered multiple injuries that required many operations and a two-year-long period of intensive rehabilitation. During her rehabilitation the question, ''Why am I alive?'' haunted her.

Marianne embarked on a search for an answer to her question. She saw a psychotherapist and began studying the literature about near death experiences. She says, ''For a long time after the accident I wondered why I didn't die. Naming my genius gave me a partial answer. I believe my genius is the energy of my soul, and I know at a very deep level that there is more I must do with that energy.''

Marianne calls her genius Preparing the Way.

Andrea's and Marianne's conclusions demonstrate two possible beliefs about genius. Andrea believes genius is the product of nurturing, while Francine's view is entirely spiritual. Which is correct? I do not know the answer in any way that can be proven. It may be that Andrea is entirely correct and Marianne's belief arises out of her need to find an answer to a haunting question. It may be that Marianne is correct and Andrea recalls her dousing because it was a violation of her genius.

My own beliefs are more like Marianne's.

Tools for Understanding Your Genius

Decide which of the following ways of thinking about your genius makes the most sense to you right now. Don't seek the ''right'' answer. Allow yourself the luxury of an intuitive guess.

The beliefs are not mutually exclusive and you may be attracted to aspects of more than one belief. If so, feel free to write a statement of your own beliefs about genius. Remember that your understanding of genius is not a problem to be solved but a mystery to be explored. There is no right answer; there are only your beliefs.

- Core Process: Your unique way of processing the data that the world provides to produce a desirable outcome
- Natural Power: An ability or capacity that comes naturally to you and toward which you are strongly inclined
- Greek and Roman Genius: A spirit that was born at the same time you were, that attends you throughout your life, acting as both guardian angel and guiding star
- Soul's Energy: A positive, purposeful force at the core of your being

4

Frustration and Curses

Your self-expression is your gift to the world.

—LAURENCE BOLDT

The beginning of chapter 2 recounts the story of Werner Heisenberg's discovery of the uncertainty principle of quantum mechanics. Before his walk in the Copenhagen park, his inability to solve the problem before him had left him frustrated. He described himself as "utterly exhausted and rather tense." His frustration arose because his genius was stymied.

Frustration is the experience of feeling thwarted. It occurs when your conscious plans or unconscious agendas seem defeated. You feel baffled and, perhaps, useless. Frustration visits you when what you are trying to do isn't working. Hans Selye, who is best known for his research and writing about stress, says,

Blocking the fulfillment of man's natural drives causes as much distress as the forced prolongation and intensification of any activity beyond the desired level. Ignoring this rule leads to frustration, fatigue, and exhaustion which can progress to a mental or physical breakdown.

You have no more natural a drive than your genius. Frustration is very often a clue that circumstances or other people are blocking fulfillment of your genius, or you are prolonging and intensifying your genius beyond the level that is wise. If you notice your frustration early, before it progresses to fatigue, exhaustion, and breakdown, and if you determine the source of your frustration, you may gain valuable clues about your genius.

Joyce: Digging Deeper

As Selye points out, there is a second path to frustration besides having our natural drives blocked. The other path is prolonging and intensifying an activity beyond the level that is healthy for us. Joyce's experience in her marriage illustrates this second path to frustration. Joyce and her husband have been married for twenty years. Her genius is Digging Deeper. Here is how she describes it:

When I get involved in something I really sink myself into it. I want to be part of everything there is to do with it—

the big picture, the meaning of the whole thing, the details, the day-to-day of it, everything. I think about whatever it is constantly. I want to talk about it all the time, and I want, always, to find some deeper meaning for what is happening. I get totally involved. Whatever it is can become a religion for me.

Joyce's attempts to dig deeper about problems in her marriage created years of frustration for her.

She said, "The problem was that I wanted to dig deeper about the marriage and my husband wouldn't. My struggle with that difference between us produced nearly twenty years of frustration and bizarre behavior on my part."

Unlike Francine, who chose to leave the company she worked for, Joyce chose to remain in her marriage. Joyce realized that the primary source of her frustration was that she chose to dig deeper into external things like her marriage and her work.

She said, "When I focused on digging deeply first and foremost in myself, the problems I was having with my marriage and my work went away."

Joyce moved away from the home that she and her husband shared and rented an apartment where she lived alone for eight months. She had to learn about herself. Only then could she dig deeply into other things without losing her sense of who she is.

Catch It Early

The trick in noticing frustration and using it to name your genius is to catch yourself feeling the frustration early in its life. For example, as I write this I am also wondering about a close friend. I expected to talk with her by phone four days ago. I have called six times in those four days. My friend has an answering machine, but that seems to be inoperative. She has not called me, even though our agreement was to try to reach one another. She lives with a friend, but neither of them have picked up the ringing phone at the other end of the line.

As I have said, my genius is Creating Clarity. Talk about a situation without clarity! Is my friend injured? I am certain she is not angry with me. I have a mix of emotions: concerned, alarmed, and frustrated. Noticing my frustration, I ask, "What is it about myself that is being thwarted?" The answer: What is being thwarted is my drive to be clear about what is happening. The ambiguity of the situation is frustrating because my genius craves clarity. There is the clue uncovered.

Frustration is not always a clue to the workings of your genius, however. For example, you may also feel frustration when learning a new skill or when trying to solve a difficult problem. This type of frustration may or may not have anything to do with your genius.

Examine It Quietly

To examine your frustration for clues about your genius, identify several situations about which you feel frustrated. They might be large issues or small incidents. They might be from the distant past, perhaps when you were a child, or they might be recent. Perhaps there is some frustration alive for you right now. Sit quietly and recall the details of one of the situations. It may help to close your eyes as you do that. Do this for each of the situations, asking after each period of recollection, "What is it about myself that was thwarted in this situation?" Don't try to force the answer; if it doesn't come to you in a few minutes, go on to another situation. If an answer does come, go on to recall other situations or review situations you recalled before the answer came. See if the answer fits those other situations.

Curses

Frustration is something we would rather avoid, but it proves to be an important clue to our geniuses. There is yet another thing we would rather avoid that is also often an important clue: the curses that other people lay at our feet.

As a small child, Cheryl was called "curious" by her proud parents. She was one of those chidren about whom we say, "She is into everything.'' No closet door nor kitchen cabinet went uno-pened. No pot nor pan, no cardboard box went unplayed with. No toy nor household gizmo went unexplored.

In school all subjects delighted her. Art and mathematics were both exciting arenas.

Then it came time to choose a college and a college major. Cheryl was vaguely disturbed by having to make such choices. She wanted to see many college catalogues and visit as many campuses as she could. She could not settle on a major; many seemed ap-pealing.

Her parents became frustrated with her. Now her curiosity was inconvenient to them. They wanted a decision. The child who once was ''curious'' had become a teenager who was ''unfocused'' and ''unable to commit.''

Cheryl's genius, which she calls Exploring All Avenues, no longer pleased her parents. What once delighted them about her now seemed a curse.

We pin many negative labels, what I am calling curses, on one another: unfocused, unable to commit, bossy, loud, shy, waffling, flighty, intense, compulsive, and so on. These negative labels can be important clues to our geniuses if we can identify what it is about us that was inconvenient or caused discomfort to those who gave us the label.

I suggest that, after using the following tools, you put this book down for a day and go on to something else. Give yourself a day of noticing what you do when you are not noticing what you do, noticing your frustration, and exploring the negative labels others have pinned on you.

Tools for Noticing Your Frustration

• SOURCES OF FRUSTRATION

Complete these sentences, then examine your words for connections or patterns.

*I feel frustrated when*_____.

*I feel frustrated when*_____.

*I feel frustrated when*_____.

*I feel frustrated when*_____.

*I feel frustrated when*_____.

_____ *frustrates me because*_____.

_____ *frustrates me because*_____.

_____ *frustrates me because*_____.

*Sometimes, when I am frustrated, the thing about me that is being thwarted is*_____.

*Sometimes, when I am frustrated, the thing about me that is being thwarted is*_____.

*Sometimes, when I am frustrated, the thing about me that is being thwarted is*_____.

As a child or teenager, I felt frustrated when_____.
As a child or teenager, I felt frustrated when_____.

• NAME TAGS

During workshops about genius I ask the people attending to wear name tags with their best current guess about their genius on the tag. This device encourages attention to the genius. It also allows people to metaphorically try on a name, wear it for a while, and see if it feels right.

I don't imagine you will want to go about your daily life wearing such a name tag. However, if you have some inkling of a name for your genius, write it on a piece of paper and tape it somewhere that you will notice it. Change it as often as a new possibility comes to mind. As you look at it you may notice yourself thinking, "That's not right." If so, trust that impulse and keep searching for a name.

• NEGATIVE LABELS

List negative labels others have given you. Ask yourself, "What was it about me that annoyed them or was inconvenient for them?" Try to frame your answer in a positive way, rather than as a criticism of yourself.

5

Telling Stories

There is no off position on the genius switch.
—DAVID LETTERMAN

It is half-past seven in the morning, and the June air is already steamy in the small nature preserve near my home. I have just recently discovered this place, and have begun to visit it. I sit on a wooden bench, sipping coffee, seeking whatever lessons the Little Miami River has for me. The river makes its way through the forest about ten feet beyond the bench. In the past few days, the river has cleared itself of the brown muddiness it carries after heavy spring and early summer rains, and its new emerald green clarity reflects the canopy of broad oak trees that surround and shade me.

The crack of a fallen twig calls my attention to a man walking the narrow trail that leads here, approaching my riverside haven.

He is wearing heavy, scuffed shoes, a well worn black and yellow plaid work shirt, faded khaki pants. He has not shaved recently; a gray and black stubble covers his jaw. I guess that he is in his sixties. He smiles as if to assure me that he is an OK fellow.

"River's getting back to normal," he says, stopping behind the bench, peering over my shoulder and through the trees at the slow-moving water.

I am not sure that I want conversation just now, so I murmur a reluctant, "Yes."

"A few weeks ago," he says, "It was so high it covered that bench you are on."

He sits down and I know that if I don't want conversation, I will have to leave. I decide to stay.

He extends his hand, "My name is Clyde. Haven't seen you here before."

I introduce myself. "So you come here a lot?" I ask.

He says, "Yes. I hang out here since I got laid off a few months ago. I needed something to do so I volunteered to take care of the park. I open the gates in the morning, hang out most of the day, go home for dinner, then come back until its time to close the gates at sundown. It keeps me busy and I like it here."

During the few times I have been here, I have not noticed Clyde. I now feel sure, however, that he has noticed me and is curious about this newcomer to his park.

I ask questions, he answers, and in the course of about ten

minutes I learn that he was a maintenance man in a warehouse, that he lives with and cares for an elderly sister, and that he owns two rental properties.

As he tells these stories, I begin listening between the lines for clues to his genius. It is an amusing game, and one that I can't seem to stop because I am writing this book.

I begin to think that his genius has something to do with taking care, or perhaps it is about fixing. Maintenance work is, after all, taking care of something or fixing something. He spends his time now caring for the park, he takes care of his elderly sister, whom he describes as "not right," and he does most of the repair work on his rental properties. He is taking care, fixing, maintaining, making things right, and so forth. The thought occurs that, if I were to have trouble with my car as I leave the park, Clyde would be right there to help out.

Although I cannot say how Clyde would name his genius, I am certain that many clues lie within the stories he is telling me.

At the end of the last chapter I suggested that you begin noting words that might become part of your name for your genius. This chapter describes a technique for generating more words. The words that you generate in this technique will provide you with the raw material for naming your genius.

The technique involves telling stories about yourself. You will then search the stories for the clues to your genius, much as I searched Clyde's stories for clues to his.

There are four steps in this storytelling process. You will need your journal or some other writing material.

Step 1: Tell Three Stories

Think about three instances in your life when you were successful, you felt good about yourself, and whatever you were doing just seemed to flow. "Successful" means success by whatever criteria you chose. "Felt good about yourself" means that you felt a sense of accomplishment and rightness about whatever you were doing. "Just seemed to flow" means that things came easily and naturally to you; there was little or no struggle. These three instances can be from any period in your life. They might be about a childhood experience, about your work or hobbies, or about something you did with your family. They might be singular spontaneous events or processes that occurred over a longer period of time. There are no restrictions except,

1. You were successful,
2. You felt good about yourself,
3. Things just seemed to flow naturally.

After you have identified those three instances, write about eight or ten sentences that describe the instance. When you are writing, focus on what you actually did, not on what other people did nor on the circumstances surrounding the event. Use the word "I" frequently to describe your behavior, thoughts, and feelings. Do not write a description of the event so much as a description of yourself as a part of the event.

For example, here are the three stories I wrote when I was trying to name my genius:

In the mid-seventies I worked for a consulting firm whose purpose was to provide services to nonprofit corporations and educational institutions. The services involved training drug counselors, teachers, and medical practitioners about what we called humanistic education or values education. I designed training programs, taught, and facilitated groups. I planned projects. I was part of a team of people, and I learned a great deal from the other team members. I also enjoyed myself.

When I was maybe nine or ten years old, I remember that I got a toy printing press for my birthday. It had rubber letters that fit into a machine with a drum on it, and ink. My family had just moved into a new neighborhood, and I created a neighborhood newspaper. That would give me an excuse to interview people who lived there. I wanted to understand more about who they were and what had gone on there before we moved in. I interviewed people, wrote about what they told me, and printed what I wrote.

My ex-wife and I owned two horses. They were both jumpers. She was an avid rider and had been since she was a little girl. It was mostly all new to me. While she took jumping lessons, I preferred a casual trail ride through the woods. I did watch her lessons though, and I guess I learned a lot just from watching. Once, her teacher coaxed me into the ring and set up a low jump. I climbed aboard, the horse and I did a slow canter once around the ring, and we took the hurdle perfectly. There were three or four people around, and they all cheered. I was amazed, and the next week I began lessons myself, learning more about jumping and becoming pretty decent at it.

Step 2: Create Two Lists

Create two lists from the words you used to describe the three situations you wrote about. The first list is a list of verbs that you used to describe your own actions. Usually these will be the words immediately following the word "I." For example, in my first story I wrote, "I designed training programs." The word that goes on this first list is "designed."

The second list will contain words or phrases that describe

what it was you acted upon. For example, I designed "training programs." Often, but not always, this list will contain the objects of the sentences you wrote beginning with "I." In some cases the object is not present in the sentences. Don't be concerned about that; the purpose of this exercise is to generate words, not to become a grammarian.

Here are my two lists:

Verbs *(Actions I Took)*	Objects *(What I Took Action On)*
worked	for consulting firm
designed	training programs
taught	
facilitated	groups
planned	projects
learned	a great deal
enjoyed	myself
created	newspaper
interview	people
wanted	understand more
interviewed	people
wrote	what they told me
printed	what I wrote
preferred	trail ride
watch	lessons
learned	a lot

climbed	horse
did	canter
took	hurdle
was	amazed
began	lessons
learning	more
becoming	decent

Step 3: What Attracts You?

Review your lists, and circle the words or phrases that appeal to you. Don't concern yourself at this point with why the words appeal to you, just notice whether, as you look at each word, you feel some attraction to it. From my list of verbs I chose:

designed

taught

facilitated

planned

learned

enjoyed

created

interview

interviewed

wrote

learned

learning

becoming

From my list of objects I chose:

groups

projects

people

understand

people

lessons

lessons

more

Along with my notes about noticing and about frustration, the words in these lists were the raw data I had at hand for naming my genius.

Step 4: Find the Common Denominator

Your genius is the common denominator about your own energy that lies within the stories you wrote. In mathematics, a common denominator is the number that a series of numbers can be divided by. However, I do not mean "common denominator" in the literal and mathematical sense. In order to make this notion of a common denominator come alive, find the common denominators in each of these three lines of numbers:

4, 6, 12, 24, 100

9, 15, 21, 30

15, 25, 65, 90

The common denominators are 2, 3, and 5.

Finding the common denominator in the stories you wrote is not quite so simple, however, because this common denominator lies beneath the surface data. It is not your ordinary common denominator. As an example, find the common denominator in this line of numbers:

2, 10, 13, 29, 35, 300

The common denominator for this line of numbers is that the word corresponding to each number begins with the letter "t."

Two, ten, thirteen, twenty-nine, thirty-five, three hundred.

The common denominator lies beneath the surface of the numbers themselves. It is not obvious, just as your genius may not be obvious in the lists of words you created. You will have to dig for it; dig underneath the surface information, just as you had to dig to find the "common denominator" in the last row of numbers.

Congratulations if you got the answer to the last row of numbers. Most people do not.

Primary Intent

Chapter 3 described genius in four different ways; as a Core Process, a natural power, the energy of the soul, and the ancient Roman idea of a spirit that attends you. There is a fifth way of thinking about it that will help you make sense of the lists you generated. You can also think of your genius as the primary intent behind the skills and activities on your lists. Your genius is a natural power that seeks expression. The skills and activities that attract you are those that allow expression to your genius. These are also likely to be the things you do best.

Thinking of your genius in this way provides another way of discovering it. Review your lists again and add any skills or activities you enjoy. For example, the skills and activities I enjoy are teaching, writing, photography, doing research, designing training programs, fishing for trout, counseling, and consulting. When I ask myself, ''What is the primary intent behind all of those skills and activities?'' the answer is that I enjoy them because they are all, in one way or another, about creating clarity, either for myself or for others.

Unless I am fully aware of my genius, I believe the primary intent of counseling or consulting is to help others, and I believe the primary intent of doing research is to gain new knowledge. Those are, however, merely my conscious intentions of the moment. My primary intent, which is creating clarity, lurks underneath my conscious intent.

The connection between the skills and activities you enjoy the most and your genius is not always obvious. Notice that I put fishing for trout on my list. While I love hooking and landing a good fish, I don't much mind coming home with an empty creel as long as I have had a good time. A good time means that I have been actively working at what I enjoy most: creating clarity about the business of fishing for trout. New clarity is more important to me than a trout. Each river is a new experience each day; an experience that begs me for clarity.

The final step to name your genius is using all the information you have generated throughout the last three chapters. In the next chapter I will tell you about how other people have approached this important step.

Crucial Questions

So far, I have offered many questions you might ask in your attempt to name your genius. Out of all those questions, there are four that are crucial. I will list those four questions here as a handy reference.

1. What is the connection between all of the things you notice about yourself when you are not noticing yourself? Another way of saying this is, "What is the common denominator?"

2. When you are feeling frustrated, what is it about you that is being thwarted?

3. What unique and special gift do you give yourself continually and also offer to others?

4. What is the primary intent behind the skills and activities you most enjoy?

There is one answer to all four questions: it is your genius.

Tools for Examining Your Stories

WHAT IS GENIUS?

I have added another way of thinking about the concept of genius to the list in chapter 3: Primary Intent. Also, your ideas about what this thing we are calling genius really is may have changed after the last few chapters. It may be useful to revisit the list.

Decide which of the following ways of thinking about your genius makes the most sense to you right now. Don't seek the "right" answer. Allow yourself the luxury of an intuitive guess.

The beliefs are not mutually exclusive and you may be attracted to aspects of more than one belief. If so, feel free to write a statement of your own beliefs about genius. Remember that your understanding of genius is not a problem to be solved but a mystery to be explored. There is no right answer; there are only your beliefs.

> *Core Process: Your unique way of processing the data that the world provides to produce a desirable outcome*
>
> *Natural Power: An ability or capacity that comes naturally to you and toward which you are strongly inclined*
>
> *Greek and Roman Genius: A spirit that was born at the same time you were, which attends you throughout your life, acting as both guardian angel and guiding star*
>
> *Soul's Energy: A positive, purposeful force at the core of your being*
>
> *Primary Intent: The underlying motive of the talents and skills you develop and practice*

A CARD GAME

On index cards, write the words that appealed to you from the storytelling exercise described in this chapter. Write one word per card. Place all of the cards on a table. Begin moving them around. Do they form groupings? Do some words seem similar to you? In what way?

THE COMMON DENOMINATOR

Look at the lists of words you created while reading this chapter. Make a list of the common denominators for those words.

6

Solving the
Puzzle

The orderly and wise soul follows its guide and
understands its circumstances.

—PLATO

Now you will turn the information you generated in the previous chapters into a name for your genius. I know of no tried-and-true method for doing this; remember that naming your genius is an Aha! process and not one that lends itself to intellectual analysis. It is like putting together a complex jigsaw puzzle. You now have many pieces of the puzzle: your notes about noticing yourself, your notes about what is being thwarted when you are experiencing frustration, the words from your stories, and your notes about the primary intent behind the skills and activities you enjoy. The trick is seeing how the pieces fit together.

I can explain my process, but it won't necessarily be the same for you; it amazes me how many different ways people invent for arriving at a name for their genius.

I looked at my lists and noticed that the words "learned," "created," "understanding," and "lessons" seemed to be similar; they seemed to be about the same thing. "What are those words about?" I asked. I also noticed that the words "designed," "taught," "facilitated," "planned," "interviewed," and "wrote" described activities I performed in order to produce learning, lessons, and understanding. The words began taking two shapes for me. The first shape was a group of concepts having to do with learning. The second shape was a group of concepts having to do with methods of learning or communicating what I have learned. I also noticed that most of my frustration arose from not understanding events or what people told me. Pieces of my puzzle were beginning to come together.

I began to suspect that my genius had something to do with understanding and communicating. Remembering the rules for naming my genius, I knew that my name could contain only one verb. I also suspected that understanding and communicating were not my primary intent. I asked myself, "What is my primary intent underneath understanding and communicating?" The answer was "producing clarity," but I didn't like the term "producing." I looked at my list again and the word "created" jumped out at me. Then the words "creating clarity" burst into my mind like a blinding light through a door that sprang open at that moment. There was the Aha! My genius is Creating Clarity.

It all sounds so simple in the retelling, but it wasn't simple at all. The story I have just told is a bit like saying, "I solved this five-hundred-piece jigsaw puzzle by first concentrating on the red, then the blue, then the edges, and finally the middle." In truth, the process took several weeks and was filled with questioning, false starts, and confusion. Just like doing a five-hundred-piece jigsaw puzzle.

How to Solve a Five Hundred–Piece Puzzle

The best advice I can give you about naming your genius is the same advice I would give about putting together a five-hundred-piece jigsaw puzzle. First, examine the pieces to see which ones seem to go together. In this case the pieces are the words in the lists you just created, what you have noticed about yourself, and what you have learned from your frustration. Second, when you find a few pieces that go together, ask yourself what they mean. What do they have in common? How do they fit together? Third, keep looking at the loose pieces to discover more pieces that fit together or to see if they relate to the pieces that are already together. If they don't go together or don't fit what you already have together, set them aside. Fourth, if you don't seem to be getting anywhere, walk away for a while. Give your unconscious a chance to break through the clutter in your conscious mind.

Trusting your intuition is also an important part of naming

your genius. Here is what I mean: I am sitting at my word processor, thinking about what I want to say, and getting the words out. I stop for a moment and a seemingly extraneous thought enters my mind. One way of dealing with that thought is to banish it. A second way is to ask myself, "I wonder what that thought has to do with my writing?" Sometimes the thought is in fact entirely extraneous, like, "I forgot to pick up the laundry." Often the thought leads me into an area I need to explore in my writing.

As you seek a name for your genius, trust those seemingly extraneous thoughts long enough to find out what they mean. Ask, "What does this thought have to do with my genius?" These thoughts will most likely come to you during a break in the conscious work of discovering a name. Mike's experience is a good example of how getting away from the conscious work of naming your genius can be productive.

After I generated my stories, the information was just sitting there, and I wasn't able to bring any focus to it. The next morning I went for a run. When I run, I like to let my intuition wander. I can even remember visually, although it has been almost ten years, the place where I was when the words Discovering Deeper Connections hit me. It seemed that those words crystallized something that was essentially me.

Remember as you try to find the right name that the lists you created are merely raw data. The actual words to describe your genius may be in the lists, but it is equally likely that they will not appear there. Also be aware that, unlike a five-hundred-piece jigsaw puzzle, your genius does not come in a box with a picture of itself on the cover, so your task may be a bit more challenging.

The Moment of Discovery

Many people who have discovered their genius recall the moment of discovery vividly, and there is a lot to learn by examining some of those moments.

Diana's moment of discovery was quite dramatic. Diana is a colleague of mine who calls her genius Taking Care. Her process of arriving at that name is instructive in several ways. She learned about noticing and frustration, completed the exercise about telling stories, talked to several people who know her well, and named her genius Taking Charge. She told me that the name Taking Charge seemed to fit her. She is wonderful at organizing. When she leads a workshop, she looks to see what needs to be done, then does it. When I say to her, "We need to get this done by Friday. Can you take charge of it?" I know that if she says, "Yes," it will surely get done by Friday.

But something nagged at Diana. She told me, "The name Taking Charge feels pretty good, but I don't get excited about it. It is true about me, but I sense that I am missing something. I am still thinking about it, and I don't know why I am still thinking about it.''

We talked about her discomfort for a few moments, then went on to discuss other things. She expressed her surprise about something a friend had said: that he admires how Diana takes care of herself. She said to me, ''I was surprised to hear this remark. I never thought about taking care of myself. But when I examined it, I realized I do. I take great care of myself. I limited my traveling because it was too stressful. I work out regularly. I get my hair and nails done every week whether I need it or not. I put those things on my calendar and give them priority. I get help when I need it. When I wanted to spend more time at home, I gave up my office space and moved everything to my house.''

I recalled her discomfort about the name she had chosen for her genius. I said to her, ''Diana, I don't think your genius is Taking Charge. I think it is Taking Care.''

Diana is not given to overt displays of emotion, but at that moment she began to cry. Later, she described the experience. ''You talk about gut feelings! When you said 'Taking Care,' something just bubbled up inside me. It started somewhere in my gut and came straight up. What an emotional release! Taking Care just felt so right, and I felt so relieved to know myself in that way. It was wonderful. In that instant, I truly saw myself. I saw my own energy and power.''

Diana's experience of naming her genius is instructive in three ways. First, her reaction when she first heard the words "Taking Care" is one of the more dramatic examples of what I call the moment of discovery. What happened inside Diana at that moment was a knowing that goes beyond intellectual knowledge. It involved her whole self; her body, mind, feeling, and spirit. Diana experienced what Eugene Gendlin calls a "felt sense." In his book *Focusing*, Gendlin describes a felt sense like this:

A felt sense is not a mental experience but a physical one. Physical. A bodily awareness of a situation or person or event. An internal aura that encompasses everything you feel and know about the given subject at a given time—encompasses it and communicates it to you all at once rather than detail by detail. Think of it as a taste, if you like, or a great musical chord that makes you feel a powerful impact, a big round unclear feeling.

A felt sense, according to Gendlin, has these characteristics:

1. It is not a mere mental experience, but an internal body awareness.
2. It is almost always unclear at first.
3. It does not arrive in the form of thoughts or words or other separate units, but as a single bodily feeling.

4. It is not an emotion, but has emotional components along with mental components.
5. It has the power to create change.
6. When you experience a felt sense, something in your body releases, something that has felt tight lets go.

I can usually tell when another person has truly discovered his or her genius because the person's response to the discovery is physical. The physical response is evidence of the felt sense of the rightness of genius. It isn't often as dramatic as Diana's tears. Usually it shows as a large grin or smile, the kind of smile that says, "Oh my! Yes! That's it! And isn't it wonderful!"

One person described the feeling as a buzz.

Sometimes the experience is more like anxiety or fear. Joyce, whose genius is Digging Deeper, says, "When I started to get close to my moment of discovery, I didn't want my genius to be Digging Deeper. A friend talked it through with me and heard how upset I was. Finally it clicked that this is it. Some part of me didn't want to see it or was afraid of it."

The second significant aspect of Diana's experience is that the name Taking Care was not the first name she had for her genius. This is often the case. As I wrote in chapter 1, the process of naming your genius is like peeling an onion. The outer layers usually consist of skills, talents, interests, or abilities you developed to give a voice to your genius. Diana's ability to take charge and her skills at organization are the mechanisms that her genius uses to express itself. Her primary intent when she is taking charge or organizing is Taking Care.

When I was trying to name my genius, I thought of Creating Learning Experiences, Putting Ideas Together, and Seeking Truth as possible names, but did not experience a felt sense of rightness about them. Yes, I do all of those things; but I only do them in the service of Creating Clarity. Those are skills, talents, interests, and abilities that form the outer layers of the onion; they are not my primary intent.

The true test of whether the name you choose is correct lies in your own felt sense of the rightness of it. If you have chosen a name for your genius but are experiencing doubt, trust your doubt and keep searching.

Wait for the Aha! that will accompany your felt sense of the right name for your genius. When it is right, you will know, with more than intellectual knowledge, that it is right.

Remember, however, sometimes genius itself makes it difficult to name genius. If your genius is something like Considering Alternatives or Going Deeper, you will probably find a name and then want to consider alternatives or peel the onion further.

The third important aspect of Diana's moment of discovery is that she talked with other people about her genius. She used the feedback she got from others to help in her search. The friend who told her that he admired how she takes care of herself gave Diana a wonderful gift: the missing clue to her genius. When she spoke of her discomfort, she alerted me to look for further clues, help her discover her primary intent, and notice her genius contained in the very words her friend spoke to her.

The people who know you often see aspects of you that you do not see yourself. I think this is particularly true of your genius, which comes so naturally to you that you probably take it for granted and don't notice it. Joyce told me, "It is so much a part of the fabric of who I am that I couldn't see it. It was invisible to me because I experienced it as a universal thing that everybody did." In the next chapter I will tell you how to talk about your genius with other people.

Dan also got an important clue from other people. He was attending a five-day workshop that included discovering genius. The workshop contained free time for reflection, journal writing, and recreation. During one of these periods, Dan and a few others decided to rent a sailboat and sail across a nearby lake. Dan, an accomplished sailor, asked the group, "Where do you want to go?" They told him, then set off with Dan assuming the role of figuring out how to sail to the places the group had chosen. Over dinner that evening, the group talked excitedly about its experience. One of Dan's fellow sailors noted, "Dan was more interested in charting the course than actually sailing the boat."

Dan heard the words "charting the course" and knew instantly that he had found his genius. He described this moment of discovery as ''a jolt.'' He recognized immediately how he goes about charting the course at work, in his family life, and in his career.

Mandy: Making It Work

Sometimes the moment of discovery is simply one step along a longer path. Occasionally, genius reveals itself very slowly and in stages. Mandy, the training manager for a large corporation, peeled back the onion to reveal her genius over a period of five years. She began during a workshop, when she first named her genius Opening Doors.

''The name Opening Doors came mostly from the work I do,'' she said. ''I liked putting ideas or activities on the table when I thought they had potential to change something in somebody's life. My thrill was in making the opportunities available to other people. I didn't have an enormous need for people to embrace what I was offering them. I merely wanted to open doors for people to see things in new ways and to grow. Opening doors was like planting seeds that other people would have to nurture.''

Over the next year Mandy felt nagged by the feeling that the name Opening Doors was not quite right, that there was something more, something she could not quite grasp.

''Opening Doors did not account for the depth to which I put myself into whatever I am doing, and the passion I bring to the things I am involved in,'' she said. ''For example, I am never a mere member of the professional associations I join; I am a board member, president, or committee chairperson. In my personal life, when my kids went to nursery school, I volunteered a day a week. I was in a difficult marriage, and I opened doors by bringing home the next book, the next couple's workshop announcement, the next motivational tape, or by finding the next therapist.''

About a year after the workshop, Mandy took the name Immersing Myself for her genius. She viewed her frustration over not being able to engage her husband in improving their relationship as a clue that Opening Doors was not precisely the right name for her genius. She had to peel the onion further.

She said, ''When I thought of the name Immersing Myself, it did more to explain the pain I felt over not being able to get my husband engaged in our relationship with any intensity. Opening Doors did not explain my frustration about that, and that name just felt more and more hollow to me.''

Mandy used the name Immersing Myself to describe her genius over the next four years. ''I still see a lot of truth in that name,'' she now says. ''But, I noticed that there were lots of things that I was involved in without immersing myself. I also noticed that I am not a detail person except when the issue I am working on is important to me and there is no one else to attend to the details. Then I will handle the details, but under duress.''

Mandy decided on a divorce, and during the year following

that decision, she came to a new understanding of her genius. "It came out of the realization that, when explaining to people why I was divorcing, I kept saying over and over again, 'I just couldn't make it work.' Then I started thinking that my genius is Making It Work. It isn't enough for me to be a casual observer of things I care about. I go into fix-it mode."

She believes this description of her genius fits snugly. "I was drawn to my work to find resources to apply to situations that don't work. Making It Work explains my work very well. It also explains how I have always been with my kids and with other significant people in my life. And it explains my former frustration in my marriage. Opening Doors and Immersing Myself are simply strategies I use in the process of making it work."

Mandy's five year exploration of her genius is not unusual. Many people find a name that fits and keep it. Others find new depths of meaning under their first chosen name. The genius has not changed, only the depth of understanding and the awareness that what we may at first take for genius is not genius at all, but a learned skill or strategy.

Miscellaneous Tools

• EXTRANEOUS THOUGHTS

Notice whatever extraneous thoughts come to mind while you are searching for a name for your genius. Treat those extraneous thoughts as possible clues to your genius.

• TWENTY QUESTIONS

Remember the game Twenty Questions? It goes like this: I think of a person, object, or event, and you have twenty questions to ask as you try to guess what I am thinking of. The questions must have "yes" or "no" answers. You can play Twenty Questions with your genius to try to uncover its name.

Sit quietly for a few minutes with your eyes closed and your journal in front of you. Imagine that your genius is there in the room with you. Then open your eyes and begin writing questions to your genius about its name. Listen within yourself for the "yes" or "no" answers, and record them as well. Trust your intuition about the answers you get. Record the questions and answers. Also record your ruminations about what questions to ask. Don't ask, "What is your name?" directly. Rather, ask questions that arise from your intuitions about your genius, like, "Does your name have anything to do with clarity?" or "Is your name metaphorical?" or "Am I on the right track?"

Conditions of the Experiment

- You do have a genius.
- You have only one genius.
- Your genius has been with you your entire life.
- Your genius is a gift you give yourself and others.
- Your genius is natural and spontaneous and a source of success.
- Your genius is a positive force.
- Your name for your genius may be literal or metaphorical, but it should contain only one verb and one noun.
- Your genius is not what you wish it would be, it is what it is.

7

Searching
Together

Each soul brings the particular configuration of the
Life force that it is to the needs of the Earth school.

—GARY ZUKAV

I am sitting in a circle with fifteen other people in a bright, oak-paneled room. Through large windows we can see snow falling gently on brittle grass and frozen earth. Each of the others is here to name his or her genius. I am here as their guide. It is Sunday morning; we have been here since Friday night.

In the time since we arrived, we have talked about genius and about noticing and frustration. They have told their stories to one another and created lists of words. They have been seeking the primary intent behind the skills and activities they enjoy. They have many pieces of their individual puzzles.

Nine of the others are wearing name tags displaying the names they have chosen for their genius. I am also wearing a name tag; it says Creating Clarity. The name tags are a device to encourage people to name their genius and to help us determine how far we have yet to go.

Marie: Exploring Pathways

At the beginning of each session, those who have changed their name tag since the last session are invited to talk about the new name they have found for their genius. Yesterday Marie wore a tag with the name Finding the Way. Today it reads Exploring Pathways. She talks of her drive to keep all options open and continually find new ones. She writes poetry and children's books. She is a potter and painter, a sculptor, gardener, and gourmet cook. She is experimenting with stencils and collage. In a more judgmental atmosphere she might be called "unfocused," "scattered," or a "jack of all trades and master of none." Here, however, we applaud her genius for its richness and diversity.

She says, "Finding the Way just didn't fit because it sounds like I am looking for the right way. That's not what I am doing at all. I think that all my pathways are right in some sense, and I want to explore them all."

Frank, who is not wearing a name tag, tells of his struggle to find the right name for his genius. He says that he seems to be getting nowhere. With a chuckle he says, "I am beginning to think my genius is Avoiding Myself."

Sam's name tag reads Talking It Out, but he tells us that he thinks the name is not quite right. He says he wants more help from the group before we finish.

Carmen also says she wants to talk more about her genius. Her name tag reads Developing Hope.

Ann, who is also not wearing a name tag, speaks: "Why is this so tough? If my genius is so natural to my being, why can't I find it? It shouldn't be this hard."

Loss of Awareness

Ann is correct; it shouldn't be hard. But often it is. Although naming your genius simply means discovering a natural aspect of yourself, it can be a challenge. The challenge results either from years of inattention to your genius or lack of respect for it by you or by the important people in your life.

Most people are unaware of their genius. There are at least three reasons for this. First, your genius is spontaneous and natural, so you don't even have to think about it. You just do it, though lack of awareness may prevent you from expressing it fully or using it to best advantage.

Second, as I pointed out in chapter 4, many of us have received negative messages about our genius. Others may say we are too smart for our own good or too sensitive and emotional or too picky or any number of other condemnations. Joyce, whose genius is Digging Deeper, has been called fanatical. Francine, whose genius is Engaging the Heart, has been called soft. Dave, whose genius is Straightening Up, has been called compulsive. I have been labeled too intense. Fanatical, soft, compulsive, and intense are somebody else's negative labels for parts of us that have great value when well understood and well used. These criticisms may lead us to deny our genius in order to gain the approval of others.

Third, your genius may cause trouble if you call it forth in situations where others do not want or value it. For example, I have sometimes tried to help people deal with their anger by engaging them in a discussion intended to create clarity about why they are angry. Sometimes the other person just wants to be angry, and doesn't want to understand it yet, if ever. I usually end up feeling frustrated in these situations, and I may also frustrate the other person. Sometimes the other person will respond by turning his or her anger on me.

It is definitely not a good idea for me to try to help someone create clarity about why he or she is angry with me. The last thing the other person wants in that situation is my clumsy though well-intentioned attempts to help him or her be clear. If you trot out your genius where it is unwelcome, and you do this too often, the responses of others may cause you to mistrust your genius. Sometimes others simply do not want your gift. Sometimes your genius is inconvenient to them.

No matter why you might ignore your genius, developing

awareness about it is one of the most potent and significant gifts you can give yourself.

Ann: Feeling Deeply

Ann continues speaking: "I am so frustrated by the invisibility of my genius."

The people in this group have learned that sharing what they notice about one another in a nonjudgmental way can be a potent favor.

Frank tells her, "What I notice about you, Ann, is that you really seem to connect with other people's emotions. You look sad when someone else is having a tough time, and you smile easily when someone else is laughing about something. When I was frustrated yesterday, you seemed to understand it completely."

"I do," Ann replies, "that is why I think my genius has something to do with other people."

I remind Ann to focus on her inner process and not on its outward manifestations. The outward manifestations are clues, but genius is an internal process. By definition, genius is an offering to other people. The question to ask is, "What is my unique offering?" I want Ann to see that she helps others in ways that she helps herself, and that her way of doing that is hers alone.

Marie agrees, saying, "The first name I had for my genius was Helping Others. I changed it to Finding the Way, thinking that my particular method of being helpful was to help others find their way. Now I call it Exploring Pathways. I explore all these pathways for myself, so when someone else is stuck I can often help them find a pathway out of their stuckness."

Trusting a hunch, I ask Ann, "What is it about you that is being thwarted right now?"

"I don't know. I can't get at it," she replies. "But while Frank was talking, I thought of my former career. I used to work as a nurse. I got out because it was tearing me apart."

Ann is paying attention to a seemingly extraneous thought, which is often an important clue about genius.

"How was it tearing you apart?" I ask.

Ann suddenly looks shocked. Her face crumples. She leans over, hiding her face in her hands. Her shoulders shake. She is crying.

"You just got it, didn't you?" I say to her.

She sits up again, tears still flowing down her cheeks.

"Yes," she replies softly, "my genius is Feeling Deeply. I am always the one who cries or laughs the most, feels the most frustrated or angry. That's why I had to leave nursing. I truly believe that I felt other people's pain. It was too much pain for me."

The room is quiet, all eyes on Ann, as a smile begins to glimmer through her tears. She sits back, relaxes, breathes a sigh.

Ann begins laughing. "It's been there all along, but because it caused me so much pain when I was a nurse, I think I tried to push it away.'' Then she exclaims, ''God! It felt good to cry!'' The rest of us burst into laughter. Ann has not only told us about her genius, she has also allowed us to see her gift in action. She cries easily and laughs easily because she feels deeply.

When the laughter ends, I ask, ''Who's next?''

Carmen: Finding the Positive

Carmen's name tag reads, ''Developing Hope.'' She says, ''This is close but not right.''

The group has told stories to one another about times when they were successful and things just seemed to flow. I ask her, ''What concepts from your stories are attractive to you?''

She looks at her notes and says, ''When I told my stories I talked about leading, about identifying opportunities, about developing people and ideas, making a contribution, and taking chances.''

''Those are all hopeful concepts,'' says Ann.

Carmen replies, ''I have been thinking that my genius has something to do with hope, but I'm not so sure.''

Ann asks her to elaborate.

''I always try to see the positive in people and situations. I get frustrated with my husband when he is feeling down. I try to get him to look on the bright side, be hopeful, see the positive. Sometimes he just wants to vent.''

Carmen is giving us clues about her genius. Her frustration with her husband is a signal that her genius is being thwarted. She wants him to feel hopeful; he wants to vent.

She says, "Hope isn't the right concept. I just want to be able to see the positive wherever it exists. Maybe my genius is Seeing the Positive."

I ask her to pick someone in the group, look that person in the eye, and say, "My genius is Seeing the Positive."

She does so, selecting Ann. We watch her reaction as she says the words. She looks dubious and uncertain. When she is finished speaking, she purses her lips, shakes her head from side to side.

"No," she says. "That's not quite right."

"What's wrong with it?" I ask.

"The concept of seeing is too passive," she replies. "I do more than simply see. Sometimes the positive is right in front of me and is there for me to see. But sometimes I have to find it because it isn't obvious."

"So is it Finding the Positive?" Ann asks.

"That's it! That's it! Finding the Positive!" Carmen is smiling broadly. She is also bouncing up and down lightly in her chair.

I ask her, "Will you turn once again to Ann and say, 'My genius is Finding the Positive'?"

Again, Carmen turns to Ann, says the words, "My genius is Finding the Positive."

She says it firmly, with conviction, and everybody, including Carmen, knows she has found her genius.

Frank: Searching for Clues

Stan, whose name tag reads Building Bridges, says to Frank, "You amaze me. You notice everything. It is often you that provides other people with the right clues. Like what you said to Ann about how she reads other people's feelings. Could that have something to do with your genius?"

Frank looks puzzled, as if he doesn't recognize this about himself. Other people nod their heads to affirm Stan's observation.

"My wife often tells me, 'You don't miss a trick,' " he says.

He also says, as an aside to Marie, who is sitting next to him, "I don't have a clue." Often, such asides, which I call "throwaways," are significant clues to a person's genius. I begin to wonder if Frank's genius has something to do with clues.

Marie asks, "What are your hobbies, Frank?" True to her genius, she is inviting him to explore another pathway.

"I photograph wildlife," he replies. "I like searching the woods for clues—tracking. The photography is really kind of secondary; it's my proof that I found what I was looking for."

I have another hunch. "Could your genius be something like Searching for Clues?" I ask. Frank is looking directly at me now and his eyes grow wide. I think I am on to something, but I know Frank must arrive at his genius himself. I will explain my hunch, but not try to convince him of its validity. It is crucial in these sessions to allow people to arrive at their own conclusions.

"You search for clues about wildlife in the woods. You have been searching for clues about other people's genius. It appears that you want others to have the gift of your clues."

I also know that these observations are outward manifestations of Frank's genius, so I ask, "Do you search for clues about yourself?"

"With a vengeance," he replies. "I read everything about self-help. I do all the exercises in all the books. I'm here at this workshop looking for clues about myself."

Frank smiles broadly, and I know he has the name for his genius. He reaches for a name tag and on it he writes Searching for Clues.

Sam: Generating Warmth

I turn my attention to Sam, who earlier had asked for more time. His name tag reads Talking It Out. He removes it.

"I know this name isn't right," he says. "It looks right because here I am talking it out again. But there is something underneath—another layer of the onion. I don't think Talking It Out is my primary intent, but I don't know what is."

Because your genius is a gift that you try to give other people, what other people get from you is often an important clue. I, for example, am trying to give you clarity about your genius.

I ask the group, "What gift do you get from Sam?"

Another group member, Tim, answers immediately. "Warmth," he says. There is a chorus of "yes" from the rest of the group.

"Well, that's why I like to talk things out with people," Sam says, "I like the warm feeling it creates between us. Sometimes it doesn't matter what we are talking about, as long as I get that feeling."

"Are there other ways you create warmth?" I ask.

"Not Creating Warmth," he replies, "It's Generating Warmth. That's better." A huge grin spreads across Sam's face, and we all bask in his warmth.

I have to be careful. My genius is Creating Clarity, so I often use the word "creating" in my hunches about other people's genius.

Returning to my question about other ways of generating warmth, Sam says, "I like to give presents for no special reason. It makes me feel warm. I like getting presents, too. I also enjoy calling friends just to say hello. You should see my phone bill." Then he laughs and explains, "This is embarrassing, but in my house I have a gas heater, electric backup heat, a fireplace, and a kerosene heater for emergencies. I guess generating warmth is pretty important to me."

Sam reaches for a new name tag. He writes Generating Warmth.

Martin: Pursuing Understanding

Martin is wearing a name tag that reads Solving Problems. He had not asked for time during this meeting to talk further about his genius. Now he says, "I know this isn't right."

While solving problems may very well be someone's genius, I suspect that Martin has not peeled the onion far enough. Solving problems can be thought of as a set of learned skills rather than a unique natural power.

I invite him to peel the onion further. "We are all in some way problem solvers," I tell him. "I wonder what is unique about your way of solving problems. I also wonder if that uniqueness doesn't enact itself in other ways in your life besides problem solving."

"What is it you do when you solve problems?" Frank asks.

Martin replies, "I get involved in as much as I can about the problem. I read about it. I talk to as many people as I can. I surf the Internet. I take copious notes. I think about it incessantly. I take long walks to ruminate. Those are the big problems, but I also love the small ones like how to organize my closet or where to put the grill on the deck."

This is starting to sound familiar to me. I suspect Martin's genius is akin to my own.

Then he says, "I just had a thought! The problems are like a medium for me, like paint is to an artist or words to a writer."

"Do you paint or write?" I ask.

"I used to do both," he replies. "I haven't for some time."

"What did you enjoy about painting and writing?"

"They start with ignorance," he says. "When I painted and wrote, I started with the idea that there was something I didn't know, something I was ignorant about, something I wanted to understand. The painting and writing were my ways of pursuing that understanding."

Marie chimes in, "Could your genius be something like Pursuing Understanding?"

"Yes," Martin says softly. The room is quiet as we watch him gaze into space.

"Yes," he repeats. "That's what the problem solving is about, too. And that is why I have thoroughly enjoyed this process of naming my genius."

Guidelines for Searching Together

I hope that in telling you about Ann, Frank, Carmen, Sam, and Martin I have given you the flavor of talking with other people as you try to name your genius. Such discussions will usually be two-way discussions, with both of you trying to help one another. Here are twelve guidelines for the discussion:

• YOU ARE THE ONLY EXPERT

Remember, first and foremost, that you are the only expert on your own genius. Only you know your true primary intent, even if you are struggling to uncover it. Resist any temptation to convince another person that you know the correct name for his or her genius. If you are correct, the other person will discover it, too. If you are wrong, you will lead him or her down a fruitless path. If another person attempts to convince you that he or she knows the correct name for your genius, but you don't experience a felt sense of the rightness of that name, ask the person to stop trying to convince you.

• NOTICE AND LISTEN

Two ways for someone else to help you name your genius are: first, telling you what he or she notices about you; and second, listening well. Likewise, you can best help another by telling what you notice and by listening well. Tell what you notice without judgment.

• LISTEN UNCRITICALLY

When you choose someone to talk with about your genius, choose a good listener; someone who listens uncritically. For example, it was important to Marie that she not be labeled a "jack of all trades and master of none."

• FRIENDS OR STRANGERS, DOESN'T MATTER

It is not essential that the other person know you well. The people who know you well have important information about you, but sometimes they have so many preconceived notions about you that they have a difficult time seeing you in a new way. They may also try hard to convince you of who they think you are instead of allowing you to go through whatever process you need to go through to discover your genius. It is rare in genius workshops for people to know one another well, yet they are consistently able to help one another simply by noticing one another, being uncritical, and listening. If you do want to choose someone who knows you well, choose a person who can do those three things.

• LOOK FOR THE PHYSICAL RESPONSE

Remember to look for the physical response that indicates the felt sense of the rightness of the name for someone's genius. The response may be a smile, tears, a look of shock or surprise, or some other reaction. It is not usually as dramatic as Ann's response. Frank's smile of recognition is more typical, so when people are trying to help one another name their geniuses, it is important that they look at one another.

• DO THE PUZZLES TOGETHER

Remember that trying to name your genius is like putting together a five-hundred-piece jigsaw puzzle. When two people are trying to help one another, it is like trying to cooperate to put two five-hundred-piece jigsaw puzzles together simultaneously. Work on them one at a time. Take turns. If you seem to be getting nowhere with one of them, go to the other for a while. If you seem to be getting nowhere with either puzzle, take a break.

• REMEMBER THE CONDITIONS

Remind one another often of the eight assumptions of the thought experiment to name your genius. They are described in detail in chapter 1. Here is a summary.

1. You do have a genius.
2. You have only one genius.
3. Your genius has been with you your entire life.
4. Your genius is a gift you give yourself and others.
5. Your genius is natural and spontaneous and a source of success.
6. Your genius is a positive force.
7. Your name for your genius may be literal or metaphorical, but it should contain only one verb and one noun. The verb should be progressive, that is, ending in -ing.
8. Your genius is not what you wish it would be, it is what it is.

• NOTICE THE PROCESS

Notice the other person's process as he or she tries to find a name. Look for signs of frustration and ask, "What is it about yourself that is being thwarted right now?" Also look for signs that his or her genius is getting in the way. If the person says, "I've got it!" but then starts looking somewhere else for it, does his or her genius have something to do with considering alternatives? Don't get so caught up in the content of the discussion that you fail to notice what is happening right in front of you.

• IT IS YOUR GIFT TO YOURSELF

Remember that what you do for other people and in your work and hobbies are outward manifestations of your genius, so they are important clues. Always, however, ask, as I asked Frank, "Do you give yourself this gift?" For example, Marie gives herself the gift of exploring pathways, Frank searches for clues about himself, and Ann feels deeply her own feelings. That is why they are able to help others do those things.

• NOTICE WHAT OTHERS GIVE YOU

Another way to help someone name his or her genius is to talk about what gift you get from that person. Sam, for example, arrived at the name Generating Warmth because Tim said he got warmth from Sam. You can ask others, "What gift do you get from me?"

• TRUST YOUR INTUITIONS

Trust your intuitions. While the group was helping Ann, she thought of her former career as a nurse. Talking about that seemingly extraneous thought helped her name her genius. Don't allow a thought to slip by.

Also, tell other people what hunches you have about their

genius. Just don't get too attached to your hunches or you may get in the way of the other person's process.

- **HAVE FUN!**

Tools For Groups

Any of the tools suggested in previous chapters can also be used in groups. A group might decide to use a particular tool between meetings or let everyone work at their own pace and follow their own inclinations. As with the other lists of tools in this book, select first those that seem appealing to the group.

TELLING STORIES

The technique of telling stories, explained in chapter 5, is particularly effective in groups. It involves these six steps:

1. Read chapter 5 to get the flavor of this exercise.
2. In pairs, one person (the storyteller) tells three stories about himself or herself. The stories are about instances in your life when

   - You were successful
   - You felt good about yourself
   - Things just seemed to flow naturally

The stories can be from any period in your life, and from any context—work, family life, encounters with friends, and so forth.

You have permission to brag about something wonderful that you accomplished. In fact, bragging is an essential aspect of this exercise.

When telling the stories, remember to

- focus on describing what you did—talk about your actions more than the situation
- use the word "I" often.

3. The second person in the pair (the listener) takes notes about the storyteller's stories on a piece of paper with a line drawn vertically down the center. At the top of the page, label the left-hand column Verbs (actions taken), and label the right-hand column Objects (what the action was directed upon).

While listening to the stories, be alert to any time the storyteller says "I . . ." The words that follow will usually go on the lists. For example, if the person says, "I encouraged others to get involved," the word "encouraged" goes in the left-hand column. The word "others" goes in the right-hand column. It isn't always that clear-cut, however, and you will have to use your judgment about some statements.

Another example: If the person were to say, "I was

proud," write the word "proud" in the left-hand column. Write nothing in the right-hand column.

The idea is to record a list of words that the storyteller uses to describe himself or herself. Don't worry too much about getting the words in the right column. It is more important to get the words down than to get them in the right column. You are listening for words that might be clues to the person's genius.

4. When the stories are finished, the listener hands the notes to the storyteller. Talk about the notes to clarify them. Also talk about any insights or hints about the storyteller's genius that arise from the stories.

5. Switch roles. The storyteller now becomes the listener, and vice versa.

6. When both people have their lists, each person looks at each word on his or her list, circling or underlining those words that seem appealing. Don't worry about why they seem most appealing. Allow your intuition to select them.

These words are part of your puzzle. Sometimes the words that describe your genius are on the page of notes. More often, however, the words will form clusters or associations that indicate there is something else (your genius) under the surface. You will have to peel the onion a bit further.

Look for the common denominators in the words on your list.

Remember to change all verbs into the progressive form, using -ing to indicate a process that is ongoing.

GIFTS FROM OTHERS

A major advantage of working with a group to discover your genius is that others can give you information that provides clues about your genius. Ask people in the group to answer the three questions below about you. Ask them to look at you with soft eyes, eyes that are observant but uncritical, rather than hard eyes, which are critical and judgmental. In this exercise you are allowed and encouraged to seek and give compliments. Criticism is unwelcome.

*What I notice about you is*_____.

*The gift I receive from you is*_____.

*I can count on you to*_____.

GOING PUBLIC

One test of the rightness of your name for your genius is to announce it to the group. Say to the group, "My genius is _____ _____." How does it feel to say that out loud? If you don't feel anything at all, then you probably have not yet found your genius. There ought to be some emotional energy. Sometimes the energy is nervousness and reluctance about being so open about such a special thing about yourself. Sometimes it is the pure joy of self-discovery. Sometimes it is the pride of announcing a wonderful aspect of yourself.

Watch and listen to others as they do this. You will soon be able to tell when a person has found the right name. For example, if the person is shaking his or her head from side to side when speaking to the group, the name is probably wrong. If the person says the sentence, then shrugs as if it were no big deal, the name is probably wrong. If the person lights up, smiles, or seems pleased just after saying the sentence, the name is probably right.

Remember that the decision about the correctness of a name for your genius and of other's names for theirs is not a matter of intellectual judgment. It is a matter of the felt sense of whether the name fits or it doesn't. Physical reactions to announcing the name to others are indicators of the felt sense.

THROWAWAYS

A throwaway is something a person says about himself or herself spontaneously, often in jest, as if the comment is an aside and not to be taken seriously. Throwaways are often clues that the genius is lurking nearby. For example, Frank's throwaway, "I don't have a clue," was a hint of his genius, Searching for Clues.

Notice other people's throwaways. They probably won't. When you notice a throwaway you can ask, "Does this have anything to do with your genius?" Often it does, and sometimes it doesn't.

Ask people to notice your throwaways, and begin noticing them yourself.

NAME TAGS

Whenever you think you might have a new name for your genius, wear a name tag with the name written on the tag. This will encourage attention to your genius; your attention as well as the attention of others. It will also allow you to metaphorically try on a name, wear it for a while, and see if it feels right in the way that some clothing feels right or doesn't.

Change your name tag as often as a new possibility comes to mind. As you look at it you may notice yourself thinking, "That's not right." If so, trust that impulse and keep searching for a name.

When you arrive at the name that seems right, you will probably feel pleased about writing it out and sticking it on yourself.

GESTURES

During a workshop similar to the one described in this chapter, one man frequently repeated a gesture with his hands while speaking of his genius. The gesture involved chopping the side of his right hand into the palm of his left hand. I noticed the gesture and, on a hunch, asked him if he thought it might tell him something about his genius. He said that the gesture was an expression of his desire to "cut through" all of the data he had about his genius and arrive at a name. He named his genius Cutting Through. While working with others about their geniuses, point out such repeated gestures.

Guidelines for Searching Together

You are the only expert

Notice and listen

Listen uncritically

Friends or strangers, doesn't matter

Look for the physical response

Do the puzzles together

Remember the conditions

Notice the process

It is your gift to yourself

Notice what others give you

Trust your intuitions

Have fun!

8

Commitment to a Mission

Being human is directed to something other than itself.

—VICTOR FRANKL

Along the road between the villages of Siggiewi and Ghar Lapsi, on the island nation of Malta, lies a collection of buildings called Id-Dar tal-Provvidenza, The House of Divine Providence. It is a home for mentally and physically challenged people conceived and created by a Maltese priest, Monsignor Mikiel Azzopardi. He is one of the most remarkable and memorable people I have ever met. This is his story, a story of commitment and mission.

During the early 1920s the young Azzopardi studied law at Malta University but switched to the study of theology when it became clear to him that he wanted to pursue his calling to the priesthood. In the late twenties he was given the opportunity to study at the Gregorian Institute in Rome. He saw this opportunity as a great honor, was thrilled to have it bestowed on him, and dreamed of the prestigious assignments that seemed sure to come his way after his graduation. He thought he was destined for greatness and for a life of prestige and service. He was, but in no way that he could have imagined.

Azzopardi was surprised and deeply disappointed when, after his studies in Rome were completed, he was ordered back to Malta in the role of a priest serving a parish.

He did not allow his dreams to die, deciding that if he was to ever get the prestigious assignment he believed was surely his, he would have to be the best parish priest the Catholic Church had ever seen.

The years passed. He taught religion in a secondary school and led retreats for teenagers. He acted as a chaplain during World War II. He chaired a committee to oversee the creation of a center of Catholic culture in Malta. He became ecclesiastical assistant of Malta Catholic Action. He traveled the countryside visiting the sick and elderly. He went on the radio with weekly broadcasts for those unable to attend mass and with a show explaining each Sunday's gospel.

He also made surprising and disturbing discoveries.

Azzopardi found mentally and physically challenged children hidden away by their families. There were children whose existence was unknown to neighbors, and children locked away during the day as their families worked in the fields or otherwise made a living.

These children touched him deeply, as did the families who hid them away, and whose shame about having them was profound.

He began to conceive of a home for the children, many of whom came from impoverished families. The children would be cared for and the families counseled.

On September 12, 1965, he spoke of this idea during a radio broadcast, *The Hour for the Sick*. When he returned to his home, a young woman stood outside the door, clutching an envelope. She had been waiting there for him for more than four hours.

He approached her, and she told him that she had heard his radio appeal for a home for handicapped children. She reached out and offered the envelope to him, explaining that it contained money that she had been saving for a vacation. She was giving the money to him instead, to start, she said, ". . . your home for the children."

Azzopardi later described this moment as a significant turning point in his life. I heard him say, "I knew that if I took that envelope my life would never be what I had expected it to be, and would never be the same as it had been." Until that moment he had not thought of the home as his.

He hesitated for an instant, deciding whether to commit himself to this idea, then took the envelope. It contained 100 Maltese pounds, about $300 dollars. He had been a priest serving in a parish for thirty years. He was fifty-five years old.

Today, just over thirty years later, Id-Dar tal-Provvidenza

consists of three villas, each housing a different age group of physically and mentally challenged individuals, and it is noted as one
of the best homes of its kind in Europe. Azzopardi, with obvious
pride, described the home.

> Beautiful airy rooms, recreation areas, chapels, gardens,
> shops and classrooms, kitchens, dining rooms, laundry
> rooms, a physiotherapy center properly equipped, and a
> large and beautiful gymnasium; an occupational therapy
> department including a pottery unit; a spacious Social hall
> for Staff meetings, reunions of parents, benefactors and
> friends, for film shows and theatricals as well as for music
> therapy and anything else that helps to keep these beloved
> "angels" happy and contented.

Azzopardi died in 1987, having devoted his last twenty-two
years to what he fondly called his "angels," the physically and
mentally challenged residents of Id-Dar tal-Provvidenza. Many
Maltese people think of him as a saint. His good friend, Lewis Portelli, wrote about Azzopardi just after his death:

> Perhaps one of his greatest achievements . . . was his her-
> culean feat in persuading parents and relatives to "take
> out" their handicapped, many times from the "hidden"
> places where they were kept. He was the one who convinced

everyone that having a sick or handicapped member in the family was nothing to be ashamed of.

Monsignor Azzopardi's Genius

My one meeting with Azzopardi was brief, and I cannot say how he would have described his genius. Lewis Portelli wrote that Azzopardi was "always looking ahead and beyond." He was a visionary who looked beyond what was and saw what was possible. He also looked beyond the rough surface of life to see beauty and wonder. He looked beyond the children's handicaps and saw them as "angels." He looked beyond the shame of their families and saw people in distress. He looked beyond whatever Id-Dar tal-Provvidenza was at any particular time and saw what it could and should become. The first residents were children. Children would become adolescents and need a different kind of place. Adolescents would become adults. He saw all of this, and Id-Dar tal-Provvidenza today consists of three villas: one for children, one for adolescents, and one for adults. When he was studying in Rome he looked beyond that period toward a new assignment. And, when he was assigned to serve a parish on Malta, he immediately began looking beyond that assignment as well.

Was Azzopardi's genius Looking Beyond? I suspect it was, or something quite like that. Perhaps he would have used different words.

This is speculation; I tell Azzopardi's story not so much as a story of genius, but more as a story that will help us explore commitment and mission.

Commitment, Mission, and Support

Chapter 1 introduced four core principles for making good use of your life:

1. You have a genius, which is your unique and special gift to the universe in general, and to those around you in particular.
2. A good use of your life requires following your genius.
3. A good use of your life requires commitment to a mission.
4. Following your genius and committing to a mission are aided significantly by surrounding yourself with support.

The preceding chapters contain the exercises and information you need to discover and name your genius. Your genius is a form of energy, the energy of your soul, the energy that is your unique gift to the universe, the energy that is central to your being. That energy exists for a mission that can be fulfilled only through the commitments you make. These commitments give expression to your mission in life.

Victor Frankl said it this way:

Everyone has his own specific vocation or mission in life to carry out a concrete assignment which demands fulfillment. Therein he cannot be replaced, nor can his life be repeated. Thus, everyone's task is as unique as is his specific opportunity to implement it.

The following diagram shows the relationship between genius, commitment, and mission. These three elements are surrounded by a galaxy of starlike figures. These represent elements of your personality and of your life conditions that will nurture your genius and commitments and support you in fulfilling your mission.

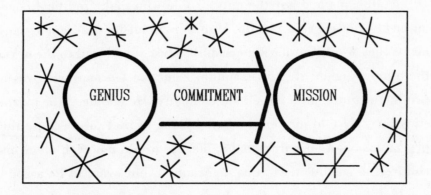

In the remainder of this chapter and in the following chapters, you will examine what role commitment plays in your life, gain clues to your mission, and discover how better to support yourself and find supportive life conditions.

Levels of Commitment

Commitment is the act of devoting yourself to something or someone. There are four forms of commitment. One form occurs when you commit to something only because it may bring you something else. This can be called political commitment, and is the shallowest form. Political commitment is on public view every day as politicians commit to promises they have little or no intention of keeping or know they can't possibly keep, in order to gain office. We all know many examples. This commitment is short-lived and may also be cynical and manipulative.

Politicians are not the only people who make political commitments, however. We all do. Managers in business accept assignments they would rather not accept because it will lead to the next, the plum assignment. For example, I once met a man who was a product manager in a large food company. He managed the pizza-stick line. He told me that he hated being in that job because the pizza sticks had no nutritional value. He would not even allow his children to eat them. He was determined, however, to be a good product line manager because he was certain that his next assignment would be a better one.

Marriage can be a political commitment. This occurs, for example, when the marriage is made because one partner wants to have children. That partner's commitment to the marriage is political because the marriage is merely a means to an end.

This is much the same decision that Azzopardi made when he returned to Malta after his period of study in Rome. He returned committed to serving his parish not entirely for its own sake but in order to impress his superiors in the Church who, he believed, could not fail to offer him something more prestigious. How long his commitment remained at this level we do not know.

There are two forms of commitment that are higher than political commitment. One is intellectual commitment, wherein you commit to something because you believe it is a good idea. We all have lots of good ideas that we never act upon and ideas that we do act upon but that fail to hold our interest. A new idea comes along, and we move on.

Azzopardi, for example, thought the idea of a home for mentally and physically challenged children was a good idea, and he acted upon it by mentioning it during his radio show. The mention set other forces in motion, forces that would soon test the level of his commitment; but he did not initially view the home as his own, merely as a good idea. He believed someone ought to create this home. However, he did not imagine devoting the rest of his life to this good idea.

Another higher form of commitment is emotional commitment. When you are emotionally committed, you feel it in your guts. It arises out of emotions such as anger, fear, or love. Like intellectual commitment, which usually holds us only as long as the idea seems attractive, emotional commitment sometimes lasts only as long as the emotion is alive.

Political, intellectual, and emotional commitment are all limited forms of commitment. Political commitment lasts only until the real prize for the commitment is won, then it lessens or evaporates entirely. Intellectual commitment lasts only as long as the idea holds our interest—and we have many interesting ideas—interesting at least to ourselves. Emotional commitment holds you only as long as the emotion is alive or until you have acted sufficiently to quell the emotion.

These forms of commitment are often enough to get you started along a worthwhile path. Azzopardi conceived of Id-Dar tal-Provvidenza out of compassion for the children he found hidden away and for their families, and perhaps out of anger that such a situation existed at all. Many worthy organizations, such as Mothers Against Drunk Drivers, are begun out of emotion: grief in that instance, and perhaps rage. Many useful products and projects began with someone's good idea or strong emotion.

In and of themselves, however, political, intellectual, and emotional commitments are usually insufficient to sustain the long term efforts, the struggles and pains, that accompany the achievement of a deeply sensed mission. They do not survive the resistance that the world often offers to good ideas or to passions.

Like Azzopardi, we await the call that shifts us to another level of commitment.

The highest form of commitment is spiritual commitment. When you are spiritually committed it is because you have heard a call from your personal deity—the universe, your personal God—from some source higher than yourself. It may also come because you sense in a spiritual commitment the opportunity to be of some service to others—your community, your family, people in need, the earth—to something larger than yourself.

There is a great leap between the thoughts "This is something that ought to be done because it is a good idea (or because I have strong feelings about it)," and "This is something I will devote my life to." This is the leap between political, intellectual, or emotional commitment on the one hand, and spiritual commitment on the other.

Tools for Examining Your Commitments

YOUR POLITICAL COMMITMENTS

What political commitments have you made throughout your life? These are commitments made, not for the sake of the commitment itself, but for the sake of an external reward that the commitment offers. What political commitments engage you during this period of your life?

YOUR INTELLECTUAL COMMITMENTS

What intellectual commitments have you made in the past? These are commitments to an idea that you believe to be a good idea.

What were the results? What intellectual commitments are you mulling over or engaged in during this period of your life?

YOUR EMOTIONAL COMMITMENTS

What emotional commitments have you made in the past? These are commitments that arose out of some strong feeling such as rage, fear, grief, or compassion. What were the results? What strong feelings have you had recently? Did they prompt you into any action?

YOUR SPIRITUAL COMMITMENTS

What spiritual commitments call to you? These are commitments that seem an absolute must. They involve a mission larger than yourself.

YOUR ENVELOPE

Have you, like Azzopardi, been handed an envelope? What did you do? Is an envelope being handed to you now?

Four Core Principles

1. You have a genius, which is your unique and special gift to the universe in general, and to those around you in particular.

2. A good use of your life requires following your genius.

3. A good use of your life requires commitment to a mission.

4. Following your genius and committing to a mission are aided significantly by surrounding yourself with support.

9

Detecting Your Mission

My business is circumference.

—EMILY DICKINSON

Your mission is the specific external expression of your genius that the universe asks of you. Your mission is the earthly reason your genius exists; it is your reason for being alive on this planet, now. Your mission is the playing field on which your genius is supposed to enter the game of life. You will be more likely to feel personally fulfilled when you are directing your genius to the fulfillment of your mission. Rewards such as wealth and fame are secondary. If you ignore your mission, you will feel as though something is missing in your life.

Although your genius is not specifically about helping others, your mission is your particular service to other individuals, to your community, customers, country, tribe, company, or to the earth.

Your mission is your answer to the question, "What does life expect of me?"

Tom, who calls his genius Finding Jewels, owns and manages a business that buys and rents homes and apartments. He sees his mission as "providing good housing at reasonable cost." He finds his jewels in attractive homes and apartments at good prices and in the people who rent from him. Linking homes with people is only one way he finds jewels, however. He also likes to wander fields and forests in search of arrowheads and other treasures. Genius is less specific about its activities.

Your mission might also be thought of as your genius at work, using the word "work" in its broadest sense of vocation or calling.

Marie, whose genius is Exploring Pathways, is a travel agent among her other creative endeavors. Her travel agency prides itself on helping people find travel adventures and explorations that will be satisfying and unique. She thoroughly enjoys exploring pathways with her clients. "What is the best path for these people?" she asks herself when trying to help a client make a decision. She speaks of her mission as "providing both adventure and peace." She books mostly cruises.

I refer to my mission as "guiding development for people, teams, and organizations," and I use that phrase as a slogan on my business stationery. As a counselor, team facilitator, organization consultant, and writer, my work is to help my clients and readers gain clarity about who they are, their current situation, their options for change, and the subtleties of the change process.

An Ancient Idea

Like the idea of genius, the concept of mission in life has been with us since ancient times and has existed in many variations in many cultures. Unlike the idea of genius, however, it has become less clouded over time.

In recent years, many fine thinkers have offered us a blizzard of material about our mission in life. The material includes books, audio- and videotapes, workshops, and television programs. You will find a listing of the books I have found useful in the Resources section at the back of this book.

These thinkers use different terminology when speaking of mission. Deepak Chopra suggests that we ask ourselves how we are best suited to serve humanity. Career consultant Lawrence Boldt calls it your mission. He asks us, "What is the message you want your life to proclaim?" James Redfield, author of *The Celestine Prophecy*, calls it "the mission only we can do."

Contemporary psychotherapist Thomas Moore speaks of it as a vocation, "a calling from a place that is the source of meaning and identity." Theologian Matthew Fox also refers to vocation as our call to participate in the work of the universe. He also writes of our mission as our cosmic role.

Sam Keen calls it a spiritual calling, and wrote, "A spiritual calling involves four elements: a gift, a delight, a need, and a discipline." The gift is your genius.

Those of us who wrestle with understanding personal mission, despite our disparity of language, seem to be in agreement on at least these things:

Your mission is not something to be invented. It is, rather, to be discovered or detected in the events of your life. James Redfield wrote, "We all have a spiritual purpose, a mission, that we have been pursuing without being fully aware of it, and once we bring it completely into consciousness, our lives can take off." And Stephen Covey wrote, "I think each of us has an internal monitor or sense, a conscience, that gives us an awareness of our own uniqueness and the singular contributions that we can make." This point of agreement is important because it suggests that you ought not attempt to create a picture of what you think your mission should to be. Rather, you ought to seek information from your past and from recent events. Your mission is a calling; thus, detecting it is an act of listening rather than inventing.

Your mission is directed outward. It is involved in your activities in the world and not solely within yourself nor for yourself. If your genius is your gift to the world, your mission is the gathering during which the gift is given. Your mission is your unique form of service. Victor Frankl said, "One should not search for an abstract meaning of life. Everyone has his own specific vocation or mission in life to carry out a concrete assignment, which demands fulfillment. Therein he cannot be replaced, nor can his life be repeated. Thus, everyone's task is as unique as is his specific opportunity to implement it.'' One does not pursue his or her mission because it is self-satisfying nor because it is rewarding in the conventional terms of power, prestige, fame, happiness, or wealth. One pursues it because one must.

If you understand your mission, you can be more effective in fulfilling it, and your life itself may feel more fulfilling. Deepak Chopra says, ''Discover your divinity, find your unique talent, serve humanity with it, and you can generate all the wealth you want.'' And Marianne Williamson wrote, ''We are to do what there is a deep psychological and emotional imperative for us to do. That's our point of power, the source of our brilliance. Our power is not rationally or willfully called forth. It's a divine dispensation, an act of grace.''

A Statement of Mission

Your mission is what you are in business for as a human being. Businesses today usually have some statement of their mission, but the term is often confused with the terms, ''vision,'' and ''values.''

A vision is a description of the reality you hope to create. Martin Luther King's dream of racial equality, harmony, and justice was a vision, as was Churchill's ''world safe for democracy.'' An acquaintance of mine, a youth counselor, sees ''a country free of chronic dependence.'' Azzopardi envisioned Id-Dar tal-Provvidenza. My favorite description of a vision comes from Marion Zimmer Bradley's novel, *The Mysts of Avalon*. Bradley has the knight Lancelot say about the Holy Grail,

> It was as if a great bell called to me, far away, a light like
> to the faraway lights in the marsh, saying, "follow" . . .
> and I know that the truth, the real truth, is there, there,
> just beyond my grasp, if only I can follow it and find it there
> and tear away that veil which shrouds it . . . it is there if
> only I can reach it. . . .

Visions have that quality of remoteness and loftiness about them; the sense that they are unreachable, but we must try to reach them anyway.

Values are those abstract qualities that we prize, like creativity, security, independence, harmony, competitiveness, and so forth. Louis Raths wrote that in order to hold a value we must prize it, choose it, and act on it. Our personal values change over time. For example, as we age, we tend to value security more than we do as younger people. Mandy's story about her five-year-long journey to name her genius Making It Work provides an insight about the relationship between genius and values. She says, "I would not have invented the lightbulb. I have no drive to make technology work. Making It Work always has a human component for me. My drive is to create harmony among people." Values are the driving force behind the commitments we make; they determine where and when we commit our genius.

Mission, which is the topic we are considering, is more closely connected to the actual work we do, whether we do it in a traditional job or in a voluntary way, whether we are paid or not. Your mission is the concrete, day-to-day expression of your genius. It is why you get up each morning.

The missions of companies are often combined in an overall statement that also includes the company's vision and values and perhaps a general description of the company's strategy as well.

Personal mission statements are usually very brief: a short sentence or phrase. Here are some examples: Alan, who leads an executive placement company, says that his mission is "to create organizations comprised solely of people doing their right work." Toni, who counsels people through transitions, says that her mission is "helping others identify their truth, and serving the poor in spirit." Warren, a training manager for a large corporation, says that his mission is "actualizing the potential of others." And Maya, a massage therapist, has made a unique and deep connection between her genius and her mission. Maya calls her genius Remembering Spirit. She believes that her work involves helping people connect the energy of their spirit with their bodies. She says that her mission is "re-membering spirit," a play on the very words she uses to describe her genius.

The two most important things about your mission statement are that it ought to feel true for you, in the same way that your name for your genius feels true, and you ought to be able to remember it.

Ten Places to Look for Clues

Your mission is to be detected, not invented. Remember that there are three kinds of detective work: intuitive (the Columbo mode), logical (the Holmes mode), and experiential (the Millhone mode). All three can produce results, and I encourage you to trust your intellect, your intuition, and your experience as you create a mission statement for yourself.

One thing all detectives need to know is where to look for clues. Here are the places you are likely to find clues to help you unearth your mission. Also, since one clue is usually not enough to build a case, look for patterns among the clues you find, just as you searched for patterns in the many clues to your genius. This list of places to look for clues about your mission is followed by a series of questions to aid you in your search. It may be useful to have your notebook or journal handy as you read this list. Make notes about whatever comes to mind.

• STRONG EMOTIONS

Anger, frustration, fear, love, sadness, or any other strong emotion may be a clue to your mission.

We often feel as though we are the passive recipients of our emotions. We are not; we create them. We create the emotions we experience out of our history, values, beliefs, and thoughts. We create them as a response to something within us. Often that something is our mission, our unique calling. For example, Azzopardi took the envelope that was handed to him partly because he had long experienced strong feelings about the challenged and neglected children and their families that he found on Malta.

The trick in detecting mission through strong emotions is to avoid or minimize feeling victimized by the inevitable negative events that often provoke them and move as quickly as possible into creative action.

• WHAT OTHER PEOPLE ASK OF YOU

Toni was divorced at the age of forty-two, after twenty years of marriage. It was a traumatic event for her. She says, "I was absolutely programmed for marriage and child raising. And nice Catholic girls from Baton Rouge just don't get divorced."

Toni sought help from a counseling service that specialized in helping people who were experiencing troubling transitions like divorce and the death of a loved one.

What she learned from her counseling led her to question her programming and to seek her own truth. She says, "I literally had to ask myself questions like, 'What color do I like, really?' and 'What music do I like, really?' "

After she had passed through this difficult transition, the people who ran the agency, recognizing her strength, skill, determination, and capacity for empathy, asked her to volunteer as a counselor to others. They, like the woman who waited outside Azzopardi's door, handed her an envelope.

Nine years later, she is quite successful in her own business of counseling people in transitions and leading workshops, fulfilling her mission of "helping others identify their truth, and serving the poor in spirit."

Other people often see us in ways we do not. Often, they sense our mission when we do not.

• UNEXPECTED EXPERIENCES AND TURNING POINTS

Toni, for most of her early life, did not expect to get divorced, and the divorce itself was a significant turning point.

Alan experienced something similar. He was fired. Alan did deep soul-searching after he was fired, and this experience became a major turning point in his life.

"Actually," he says, "I fired myself. In truth, I made it impossible for my employer to keep me. It was the wrong work for me."

During his soul-searching, he thought about his work history and read and talked with experts about the nature of work. The result is his current work heading an executive placement firm, and his mission is "to create organizations comprised solely of people doing their right work."

Unexpected experiences do not automatically become turning points. Azzopardi could have said no to the envelope. Toni could have said no to the request that she become a volunteer counselor.

Alan might have felt victimized, blamed his boss, and gone on to another job failure.

• SUFFERING

Victor Frankl's system of Logotherapy grew out of his suffering in a Nazi concentration camp. Frankl believed that suffering could be a source of meaning in life if we can alter our attitude toward the suffering. Frankl wrote,

> We must never forget that we may also find meaning in life even when confronted with a hopeless situation, when facing a fate that cannot be changed. For what then matters is to bear witness to the uniquely human potential at its best, which is to transform a personal tragedy into a triumph, to turn one's predicament into a human achievement. When we are no longer able to change a situation—just think of an incurable disease such as inoperable cancer—we are challenged to change ourselves.

Maya, for example, was a victim of childhood abuse. She also recalls that, as a child, she knew deep inside herself that there was more to life than what appeared. She recalls carrying that sense throughout her life, even when she was most afraid. As a massage therapist she helps people connect their body and spirit and respect their physical being.

It seems that, in our society, we easily adopt a victimlike attitude toward suffering. Maya did for many years. It was only after much self-exploration, aided from time to time by therapists and by a support group, that she was able to transform her attitude toward her childhood suffering.

She says, "Having the courage to be a survivor and knowing that my life was more than what happens on the surface are the two major things that formed my mission."

As with negative emotions, detecting a mission from suffering requires that we avoid or minimize feeling victimized and move into creative action.

• RIVER BANKS

After Alan was fired, he took to walking daily on the banks of a nearby river. He did this for nearly six months.

He says, "In order to detect my mission I had to calm down and quiet my mind so that I could hear the small voice inside me that knew what I was supposed to do next. Walking the river, throwing sticks into the water, and watching them float away was a form of meditation."

Although your mission is to be detected from the many messages around you, some form of meditation—quieting the mind—is often valuable. Azzopardi's mission was handed to him. For most of us, however, the call is not so blatant or dramatic. We must listen to both the call from without and the small voice within. I like to believe that during Azzopardi's moment of hesitation he was listening for that voice.

• FAMILY HISTORY

Several years ago my sister and I took our septuagenarian mother to lunch on Mother's Day. In the middle of lunch, and seemingly out of nowhere, Mother asked me, "Do you ever paint?"

I had not painted in nearly twenty-five years and was surprised that she thought I might.

"I always hoped you would follow in your grandfather's and uncle's footsteps," she said sadly.

My grandfather, after his retirement from the Postal Service, created vivid oil paintings of sailing ships, harbors, and western scenes imagined from Zane Grey novels. My uncle, for whom I was named, was a graphic artist. I took a circuitous route from high school to college, spending four intervening years as an apprentice to my uncle, studying advertising design in the evenings at an art school.

During those years I discovered I was more interested in people than paint. I left my job, entered college to study psychology, and put my art supplies away, pretty much for good.

It would seem, on the surface, that my mother's aspirations to raise a painter went unfulfilled. Still, there is a clue here about my mission. As I was writing my first book, *Artful Work*, I found myself reaching back to my own past, to my art training. The book is a synthesis of my experience as an artist and as a management consultant; an attempt to integrate artistry with all work.

My experience as a practicing artist became grounding for guiding others to find the artistry in their own work.

Likewise, Maya sees her history of childhood abuse as grounding for her mission. And Tom became a property manager, which he loves, because, as a teenager, he worked for his father, who was also a property manager, and Tom discovered his calling in the work.

In *The Celestine Prophecy*, James Redfield provides another way of searching our family history for clues about our own mission. He wrote that mission is a spiritual path involving the discovery of a truth that synthesizes what your parents believed. Redfield's protagonist is searching for a sacred manuscript. Along his journey he meets a priest, Father Carl, who tells him,

> We are not merely the physical creation of our parents; we are also the spiritual creation. You were born to these two people and their lives had an irrevocable effect on who you are. To discover your real self, you must admit that the real you began in a position between their truths. That's why you were born there; to take a higher perspective on what they stood for.

Redfield's protagonist reflected that his father's life was about maximizing his aliveness, while his mother's was about sacrifice and service. The question for him became how to live a life that included both.

Father Carl tells him to look closely at what has happened to him since birth. He says, "If you view your life as one story, from birth to right now, you'll be able to see how you have been working on this question all along."

• RECURRING IDEAS

Toni once visited a monastery for a weekend retreat. When she told friends about her experience, many expressed a desire for a similar experience, but without a religious context. She is also interested in alternative living arrangements for senior citizens.

The idea that recurs to her is creating a worldwide network of senior citizen group housing arrangements that would also serve as retreat centers. The senior citizens would manage and staff the centers.

This idea has recurred many times. It is provoked by many things, such as brochures arriving in the mail announcing retreats and visits to an elderly aunt who lives alone. These recurrences have haunted Toni over many years, and she now believes she must act in some way on her idea.

Alan has, for many years, thought of writing a book about leadership. He knows the theme and has the book outlined. This recurring idea has become a stronger presence, and he is about to take a sabbatical from his work in order to write.

• WHAT YOU HAVE CREATED OR DONE

After graduation from college, with a degree in psychology, I entered a master's degree program in education, which included a teaching internship at a large suburban high school. The internship became a full-time job teaching mathematics.

The school district was building a huge high school, consolidating three schools into one. There was great concern within the community, as well as among the school board and administration, about the effects this giant school would have on its students. Would they feel lost and alienated? What might be done?

I had been studying about change in school systems. I was also eager to utilize my background in psychology; I knew I would not be too long in mathematics classrooms. My studies led me to discovery of the role of ombudsman, a kind of freelance, outside-the-mainstream, troubleshooter role. The idea appealed to me, I proposed it to the administration of the school district, applied for the role, and they accepted.

Over the next four years I counseled students individually and in groups, created a teacher-training institute within the school district, helped the local police track down runaways, sat up at night with their desperate parents, acted as a coach for several school administrators, suggested minor changes to the facility and curriculum, mediated between warring students, between warring students and teachers, or warring students and parents, and generally did anything I could think of that seemed useful in reducing the possibility that students would feel alienated from the school, their parents, one another, or their teachers. It was fun, and I accomplished a lot.

Looking back, across a distance of twenty-five years, I see how that ombudsman role, which was very much my creation, was a cornerstone for detecting my mission of guiding development for people, teams, and organizations. It was the beginning of my consulting career.

Such creations and accomplishments, no matter how long ago, contain clues to your mission.

• DREAMS AND REVERIES

Dreams sometimes express desires and hopes that we are only vaguely aware of, if we are aware of them all.

About fifteen years ago, before I understood my mission as I now do, I dreamed of sitting in an office high in a treetop, typing away at my word processor, while people lined up outside my door to speak with me.

Over the last eight years I have had two offices. The first, in the Pocono Mountains of Pennsylvania, was on the second floor of my home, which was surrounded by tall hemlocks. There was a deck outside the sliding glass doors that brought light into my workspace, and I often worked outside, on that deck, literally in the treetops. My new office, also on the second floor of my new home, has a window from which I can touch the upper branches of a tall ash tree. My life in those two offices has largely involved the writing of this book, my previous book *Artful Work*, and a set of manuals for improving teamwork titled *Assessing Your Team*.

While people are not lined up waiting for me, at least not yet, I do receive numerous calls, letters, and E-mail messages soliciting advice, requests to speak to groups, or invitations to consult with organizations.

Had I been aware that dreams often contain clues to mission, I might have understood mine much sooner than I did.

Reveries, waking dreams, may contain the same kind of clues as the dreams that visit us while asleep.

• WHAT MAKES YOU SMILE?

I knew that an acquaintance, Ellen, had recently changed jobs. At a party I asked her, "How do you like the new job?" A brilliant smile spread across her face and her eyes grew wide with joy. She went on to tell me how she felt wasted in her previous job, and how accomplished and well utilized she now felt.

I do not know Ellen well enough to speculate about her purpose, and am not in the habit of trying to detect another person's purpose at parties. But surely her smile was a clue that her new work lies somewhere very close to her purpose.

Tools for Detecting Your Mission

The following questions and techniques will aid you in detecting your mission. Do not try to answer them all at one time. Detecting your mission may take days or weeks. Like naming your genius, detecting your mission is similar to putting together a five hundred–piece puzzle. These questions and techniques will help you find the pieces.

Recall these guidelines for putting together a five hundred–piece puzzle:

1. Examine the pieces to see which ones seem to go together. In this situation, the pieces are the thoughts and recollections you had as you read the section above, your answers to the following questions, and whatever other clues you gain from the tools below.
2. When you find a few pieces that go together, ask yourself what they mean. What do they have in common? How do they fit together? Look for patterns. Seek the common denominator.
3. Keep looking at the loose pieces to discover more pieces that fit together or to see if they relate to the pieces that are already together.
4. If they don't go together or don't fit what you already have together, set them aside.

5. If you don't seem to be getting anywhere, walk away for a while. Give your unconscious a chance to break through the clutter in your conscious mind.

Here are the questions and tools:

1. What have you experienced strong feelings about lately? What did you do about the situation that provoked those feelings? Is there something you wished you had done differently? Is there something you might do now? Search your past for strong emotions, and list the circumstances that provoked them. Can you find a pattern in the circumstances? Is there a pattern within your reactions? What creative action might you take?

2. Create a list of the things that people and organizations have asked of you in the past. Is there a pattern or common denominator? Is some person or organization asking something of you right now?

3. Here is how to create a Life Line that displays the key unexpected experiences and turning points in your life. First, draw a horizontal line in the middle of a piece of paper. Label the left end of the line 0. Label the right end with your current age. The line represents your life from birth until this moment. Place an X at the appropriate place on the line to mark each major turning point or unexpected event in your life.

Here is an abbreviated version of Toni's Life Line as an example.

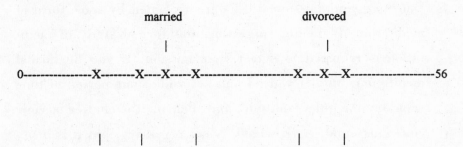

Your Life Line may have few or many points marked on it. The number of turning points doesn't matter.

Looking over all of the events and turning points on your Life Line, can you sense a pattern? Toni, for example, sees what she terms her "programming as a wife and mother," then a dramatic shift in her more recent years. It was during that shift, when she was asked to work as a counselor to people in transition, that she found her most significant clue about her mission.

4. What have been the greatest sources of suffering in your life? What has been your attitude toward the suffering? Has your

attitude provided meaning to your life? If not, what other attitude might you take?

5. Detecting your mission will be greatly aided by some form of meditation. I am not suggesting that formal study of meditation is required to detect your mission. If you do formal meditation, fine. If you do not, set aside some period of time each day for quiet, solitude, and silencing the chatter of your conscious mind. A riverbank is not necessary, but it is beneficial, as are mountains, lakes, trees, and parks. What is necessary is listening for the small voice that might reveal your mission.

6. What idea has haunted you? What might you do to move the idea forward?

7. Is there a pattern or common denominator in the work you have done? In what you have created?

8. What makes you smile?

9. Fill in the blanks below. Think about the world at large, rather than yourself, as you respond. These are, in a sense, your hopes for the world.

*Wouldn't it be great if*_____.

*Wouldn't it be great if*_____.

*Wouldn't it be great if*_____.

*Wouldn't it be great if*_____.

*Wouldn't it be great if*_____.

They are all wonderful hopes, I trust. However, you have only this life to live, and you must make choices about how to use it well. Cross off one hope. Then another. And another. Now one more. What is left?

10

Self-Responsibility
and Support

*We can change ourselves. We can change our
communities. We have incredible spirit. We can
brave life's pains and enjoy the triumphs.*

—RITA MAE BROWN

Helene was close to her father when she was a small child.
He was a stonemason, and he loved to show her his work and let
her work with him on small projects around their home. At the age
of six, Helene was pointing bricks. She began to understand what
it meant to build things.

By the time Helene was in high school, her father's business, had grown into a contracting business, and she often visited his office while he prepared estimates, ordered material,
and spoke with customers and architects. She enjoyed the atmosphere in the office and began to help out after school and during weekends.

When she finished high school, she knew what she wanted to

do with her life: She wanted to work in her father's business, and then she wanted to run it.

Helene's father died during her senior year in high school. Her older brother took over the business.

Helene told her brother of her wish to enter the family business.

"Eventually," she told him, "I would like to run the business."

He said, "No. Get married. Have children. That's the right work for a woman."

Other family members agreed with Helene's brother. Families, like other groups, are not always supportive of our being who we are or who we want to be.

Helene did get married and had four children; her dream was temporarily abandoned. She also attended sewing classes. Money was tight for her new family. Helene made most of her own clothing, made clothing for her children, and did alterations for her husband and for friends. She began to understand clothing as she had once understood building. Building clothing and building buildings were somehow similar.

Twenty years after her marriage, at the age of forty, Helene had a revelation, "Marriage isn't supposed to be slavery."

Helene told her husband that she wanted to earn a college degree in business administration. The dream of running a business was still alive in her. Her husband, much like her brother, said something like, "No. You are married. You have children. That's the right work for a woman." The result was a divorce. Because of her decision to divorce, Helene did not have the money for college.

She said, "The day my divorce became final, I walked to the end of the road that passes in front of my new home and asked, 'Now what?'" Standing there, at the end of the road, facing a barren piece of ground, she asked herself, "What do I know about?" The answer was clothing.

Helene started a small boutique, which grew into a larger boutique, which became an even larger boutique, where she not only owned the business but also the building that housed it and two apartments. Helene is a successful businesswoman.

She now says, "I loved my father's business because he helped people get what they wanted in a creative way, and a way they could afford. 'You want a brick wall?' Here is a creative brick wall. I do the same thing. 'You want clothing?' Here is creative clothing. It is clothing different from the clothing worn by the person who lives next door to you. You can't get it in the mall, and you can afford it."

What Must Change?

The starlike figures inside the diagram in chapter 8 are meant to symbolize those things that will nurture your genius, commitments, and mission. They fall into two broad categories. The first category is conditions of your life, including such things as your living arrangement, friends, family, and work; anything around you that serves as a support to your genius, commitments, and mission. The second category is aspects of your own personality, particularly your willingness to take self-responsibility.

Your genius does not exist in a vacuum. It suffers from life conditions that do not nurture it or that obstruct it, and it thrives in conditions that do nurture it. Your commitments, too, are colored by the conditions of your life, as is your ability to act on your purpose. Also, your own psychological qualities, habits of thinking, behavior, and beliefs hold the potential to nurture or obstruct the workings of your genius, commitments, and purpose. I use the term "personality" to refer to these elements.

Helene has changed the conditions of her life to better support her own sense of mission. When she first opened her boutique she found friends who were experienced businesspeople. She now surrounds herself with people who, unlike her brother and ex-husband, support her genius, commitments, and mission.

She also had to change aspects of herself. She developed the confidence that she could run a successful business without a college degree.

The conditions of your life and your own personality can be either womb or prison to your calling.

Life Conditions

Martin, like Helene, dramatically altered the conditions of his life in order to better support his genius and mission. He voluntarily left his job in promotions at a large company to start his own advertising business. He calls his genius Pursuing Understanding, and he describes his mission as "informing people about their medical options." His new business deals entirely with disseminating information about medical products.

Five years after he started his business he had ten employees, a three million dollar a year business, and contracts that ensured moderate growth. Martin poured a lot of himself into his business.

He said, "I have a lot of energy for my work because it is an expression of myself. It is like a canvas I am painting on. I want to create a masterpiece."

There is, of course, a great deal of courage involved in committing to a mission and acting on our commitments. It may feel like an unnatural act or a huge risk. Avoidance feels easier, even with the unintended consequence of feeling the sense of something missing that occurs when we avoid something we ought not avoid. This is because we don't readily connect the two—the avoidance and the feeling of something missing.

The courage involved is the courage to take responsibility for your genius and mission; to seize them boldly.

"It isn't easy," says Martin, "I stayed in my former job longer than I probably should have because I was afraid and avoided taking responsibility for who I really am."

Aspects of Personality

As with the external conditions of our lives, our own internal workings—what I am calling "personality"—can either block or nurture us. The tendencies to procrastinate, to believe we are not good enough or educated enough, to fear failure or success, to engage in addictive behavior, to fail to nurture ourselves or find nurturing others, and many other tendencies hold us back. They are all forms of avoiding our genius, commitment, and mission.

Marie, for example, whose genius is Exploring Pathways, was labeled "curious" as a child. However, as she became a teenager, then a college student, the term "curious" gave way to critical epithets such as "unfocused," "scattered," and "unable to commit." As a result she became tentative about exploring pathways that intrigued her, she procrastinated, and she began to feel that whatever she was doing at any particular moment was the wrong thing to be doing. She became highly self-critical and began to avoid activities that engaged her genius or that committed her to a mission.

Avoidance is the major obstruction we place in front of ourselves, and we have many reasons for avoiding and many ways to avoid. We can avoid setting time aside for what is meaningful to ourselves. We can avoid by encouraging distractions and interruptions, or by working compulsively, exhausting ourselves, then no longer wanting to work. We can avoid by becoming overly discouraged or overwhelmed by the tasks ahead of us. We can avoid by spending time and energy being self-critical.

Francine knew that remaining in a company that did not nourish her was avoidance. Martin avoided the risk of starting his own business for many years by wishing the people around him would change, especially his bosses. Helene, after realizing that her ex-husband would not nourish her dreams, remained married for several years, avoiding what seemed inevitable to her.

As I come near the end of this writing, I find myself wanting to avoid it more and more. Soon I will have to release this book to the world. It is a fearsome thought. My techniques of avoidance include engaging in self-criticism ("This book is boring") and the all too easy clicks of a mouse that switch me from my word processing program to a computer game. Also, for me there is a fine line between the walk among the trees that is part of the creative process, the kind of walk that might produce an Aha! experience, and the walk that is sheer avoidance. Lately, I have been taking too many walks without an Aha!

Avoiding your genius, avoiding your calling, and avoiding the commitments that will channel the energy of your genius toward your mission will produce a sense that something is missing in your life.

Self-Responsibility

The question of our responsibility for our own lives is a traditional philosophical question. It is the question of how we each create our own reality. I refer to this kind of responsibility as self-responsibility in order to distinguish it from the more common use of the word "responsibility," as in, "He is a very responsible person." Self-responsibility involves acting in accordance with your inner voice, your sense of self, your considered view about how you must be in the world. It also involves respect for your own genius and commitment to your mission. Self-responsibility is responsibility for who you are.

Peter Koestenbaum calls himself a clinical philosopher. He applies philosophical wisdom to everyday problems, business problems in particular. Koestenbaum believes that authentic self-expression arises from exploring the fundamental concerns of human existence, concerns such as death, freedom, responsibility, meaning and work, love and intimacy, identity, and so forth. He calls these our "existential ultimate concerns." He wrote, "The existential ultimate concerns, when fully understood and integrated into our lives, give us our sense of potency, energy, engagement, roots, centeredness, aliveness, joy, liberation, and hope." Koestenbaum refers to self-responsibility as the "freedom-responsibility couple," indicating that self-responsibility and freedom always attend one another. When you assume self-responsibility, you are set free of the curses of victimization and dependence.

Self-responsibility has two components: awareness and commitment. Awareness, in this context, describes the ability to make good judgments about your contribution to a situation, your impact on others, and your contribution to creating whatever circumstance surrounds you. It requires a willingness to see yourself as the source of yourself, to understand and accept that you are the creator of your own feelings, thoughts, beliefs, perceptions, and actions.

Self-responsibility, then, can be thought of as the ability to judge your impact on yourself and the world (awareness), combined with the ability to devote yourself to something or someone (commitment).

Four Orientations to Life

The following diagram shows how varying degrees of mastery of awareness and commitment lead to four general orientations toward life. These four categories do not necessarily describe types of people. Some people do live predominately in one category or the other, and I will use these stereotypes to illustrate each of the four orientations. However, most people will recognize that, at different times in their lives and under different circumstances, they have experienced all four orientations.

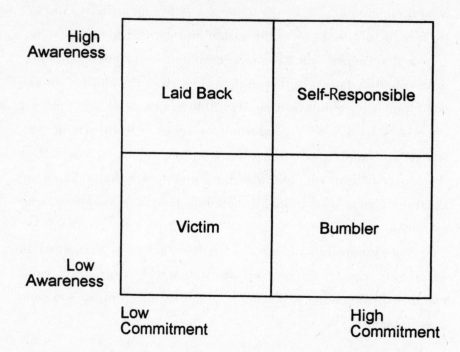

High Awareness

Laid Back   Self-Responsible

Victim   Bumbler

Low Awareness

Low Commitment   **High Commitment**

Low awareness coupled with low commitment produces a victim orientation, a sense that we are at the mercy of forces outside ourselves and are helpless to create change. It is evident in people who chronically blame others, fate, or luck and never look to themselves as a possible source of their situation or a potential agent of change, and they never do anything constructive to alter themselves or their circumstances.

Martin, for example, felt victimized by his boss and the company he worked for before deciding to start his own business. Helene felt victimized by her brother and husband. However, they did not remain in this orientation. They viewed their feelings of victimization as a clue that they ought to do something differently.

Low awareness with high commitment produces a bumbler orientation with lots of activity directed at poorly chosen commitments and no sense of how that activity affects others, situations, or oneself. The prototypical bumbler is the Jackie Gleason character, Ralph Kramden of *The Honeymooners*. Ralph is forever stumbling into impossible situations because of unrealistic plans or schemes, with little understanding of how he might be contributing to his own problems and with little insight into himself. Through the magic of television screenwriters and the wisdom of Alice, his wife, Ralph always came out all right in the end. We are often less fortunate when we bumble.

High awareness with low commitment produces a laid-back orientation, with good insight about oneself and the world, but no action, no meaningful choices. I once had an acquaintance who treated insight, in and of itself, as if it were the only key to real change in his life. He produced insight after insight about his plight but never committed to any course of action. During the five years I knew him, he remained mired in a life situation which he, himself, thought of as unfulfilling and depressing. His only relief from feeling depressed was an occasional insight.

Finally, high awareness with high commitment produces the

self-responsible orientation. People who are living in a self-responsible orientation are recognizable. They seem to be fully in charge of their own lives, seem successful, and convey an energy that infects others. They care about how others react to them but are not ruled by what others think. They move quickly beyond their feelings of victimization and minimize or eliminate any tendency to avoid. They are able to resolve problems and conflicts in ways that leave them better off, and they seem to get most of what they want. There are many stories of people acting self-responsibly in this book. Francine and Martin left unsatisfying and damaging job situations. Mandy and Toni left unsatisfying and damaging marriages. The leaving is not the important element in their stories. The important element is their drive toward taking responsibility for their hopes and dreams, their geniuses and missions.

No Blame

Self-responsibility is the antithesis of blame. When we feel ourselves blaming others, luck, or fate, we are not engaged in self-responsibility. Martin blamed his bosses for his unhappiness before he started his own company. Mandi, Toni, and Helene blamed their husbands. Maya blamed her family of origin.

Blame is a difficult issue in our society. We want to know, "Who is at fault?" If we relinquish blaming others, luck, or fate, yet hold on to the need for blame, the alternative is to then blame ourselves. Self-responsibility requires that we let go of the idea of blame altogether. When we assume a self-responsible orientation, we do not blame others; we do not blame ourselves. We merely ask, "What has happened, what is the situation, and how did I contribute?"

This does not mean that certain deeds should go unpunished. It means that, if you wish to adopt a self-responsible orientation to your life, you must move away from the victim orientation that is the source of blame.

Assuming self-responsibility means:

- Not blaming others, luck, or fate for what you are being, doing, having, or feeling
- Not blaming yourself
- Being aware of your contribution to your own life
- Committing to what you want
- Being aware of the multitude of choices you have in any given situation

Responsibility for Your Genius and Mission

Sometimes, when I lead workshops based on my book *Artful Work*, I ask people to introduce themselves to the rest of the group by naming whatever form of art they practice. If I were introducing myself, for example, I might say, "I am Dick Richards, and I am a writer." This is surprisingly difficult for many people. They experience it in much the same way an alcoholic experiences saying, for the first time, "I am an alcoholic," at an AA meeting. There is fear involved, and shame.

Once, during a break in a workshop, one of the participants told me she was a "fiber artist." I had not heard that term before and found it delightful. When the workshop resumed, I asked the people attending to name their art form. This woman said, "I sew quilts."

I asked her why she described her art differently in front of the group than she had during the break.

"Fiber artist sounds so lofty," she replied, "I didn't want to seem pretentious."

Those who find this activity difficult have told me that it involves taking responsibility for a part of themselves that they too often deny. They have denied or compromised the artist in themselves. They feel ashamed of their denial. They also fear having a valuable part of themselves revealed.

Something quite similar occurs during workshops that involve finding names for the geniuses of the people attending. The moment when they say to the group, "My genius is _____ _____," is often tense and difficult.

We often dull our awareness of our genius and mission, much as we might dull our awareness of unpleasant feelings. It is not that our genius and mission are themselves unpleasant. They will, however, provide an unpleasant feeling if we choose to avoid them or deny our responsibility for them. The unpleasant feeling is the feeling that something is missing in our lives.

Tools For Self-Responsibility and Support

- Reread the three stories that you wrote about yourself while seeking a name for your genius. Examine the external conditions in those situations. Create a list of the elements of your environment that supported you. What were the rewards for what you did? Who initiated the activity, you or someone else? Were you alone or part of a group? Was your activity primarily physical or mental? How did the people around you treat you?

- Who nurtures your genius now? Who else in your life might nurture your genius?

- What do you know about?

- What are your favorite methods of avoidance? What is it that you are currently avoiding?

- When have you felt victimized? How did you contribute to the situation? What do you do differently as a result? What awareness was missing? What commitment might you have made?

- When have you bumbled? How did you contribute to the situation? What awareness was missing?

- When have you allowed yourself to feel laid-back? What commitment was missing?
- List situations in which you acted self-responsibly or took a self-responsible orientation?
- Are you engaged in blame during this time of your life? Do you blame yourself?

Epilogue

A book ought not end with a list of tools.

As I ruminated one day about how this book should end, an image presented itself. The image is a William Blake watercolor, *Bright-Eyed Fancy*. In this painting, Blake, who often wrote of genius as an angel, painted the image of a young woman hovering above a musician who is playing a lyre. Musician Stephen Nachmanovitch says of the painting, "She is pouring out a cornucopia full of ideas in the form of pixies and babies, which the poet-musician tries to play—almost as if his lyre were an instrument for taking notes—before they evaporate into thin air." This painting is a compelling image of genius as a hovering angel that guides the musician's playing, not in a directive way but in the way of offering notes that the musician must select with his instrument. He is concentrating intently on her offerings, as if he does not wish to miss even one of them. Blake's illustration is for a poem by Thomas Gray, which includes the lines,

Oh! Lyre divine, what daring spirit
Wakes thee now?

Is this how genius works? Is my genius, Creating Clarity, offering me ideas as well? Is it up to me to concentrate on seeing them and plucking them out of the air with my computer and word processing program? Is this keyboard my lyre? What daring spirit wants to awaken me?

Does a travel agent's genius present her with brochures? Does a property manager's genius present him with buildings? Does the genius of the man who changes the oil in my car present him with the right oil? Does the interviewer I am speaking with receive questions from the cornucopia of his or her genius? I think so.

That evening, a steamy August evening in Cincinnati, as the day was on the verge of darkness, I gathered with several hundred people on a sloping tree-encircled lawn in Sharon Woods Park to hear the Cincinnati Pops Orchestra. Blake's image was still very much on my mind.

The opening number was the overture to *Orpheus in the Underworld*. I resolved to try imagining a genius with a cornucopia of pixies attending each musician. At first I had little success. It was too big a task. There was just too much going on onstage, with about forty musicians and an energetic white-clad conductor attending to their work. Also, my powers of imagination weren't yet fully engaged. I looked toward the top of the tent, thinking that the geniuses would be there, but all I noticed were moths committing acts of personal immolation around the stage lights.

During a saxophone solo, however, I could sense the saxophonist plucking notes from the air rather than creating them himself. I encountered the same sense about the pianist during the main theme from *Forrest Gump*. I was getting close.

It happened just after intermission.

Boom boom bam-boom ba-boom ba-boom ba-boom.

Boom boom bam-boom ba-boom ba-boom ba-boom.

Boom boom bam-boom ba-boom ba-boom ba-boom.

Sing, sing, sing, sing.

Everybody's got to sing.

The Cincinnati Pops is off and running. And suddenly, I can imagine them. About forty geniuses, each like Blake's and Gray's "daring spirit," hover beneath the canopy of the blue and white striped tent, cornucopias tipped to the max. Pixies are dropping everywhere. It is a pixie deluge. Musicians are furiously but deftly picking them from the air with their instruments. Not a single pixie crashes on the stage floor. They are being plucked from the air and delivered to a delighted and energized audience as individual musical notes in a frenetic exhibition by an orchestra that is really cookin'.

Suddenly the geniuses stop dropping pixies. All but one. He hovers over the drummer, cornucopia tipped, still offering his gifts.

Boom boom bam-boom ba-boom ba-boom ba-boom.

Boom boom bam-boom ba-boom ba-boom ba-boom.

Boom boom bam-boom ba-boom ba-boom ba-boom.

The drummer is unfamiliar to me. I look closely at his genius. Could it be? Yes! This genius looks like Gene Krupa. I remember Krupa's picture from an old album cover. This Krupa lookalike genius seems possessed. Sweat is dripping from him as he frantically pours pixies over the drummer on the stage. At the peak of the drum solo, the genius is reaching into the cornucopia and scooping pixies out, frantically shoving them down toward the drummer. I wonder if geniuses really sweat or if my imagination has run amok.

Tap, tap, tap-tap.

Tap, tap, tap-tap.

Tap, tap, tippety-tap.

Boom boom bam-boom ba-boom ba-boom ba-boom.

Boom boom bam-boom ba-boom ba-boom ba-boom.

Boom boom bam-boom ba-boom ba-boom ba-boom.

Each tap and each boom pours from the cornucopia, and is plucked from the air.

It happens again during the finale, *Mack the Knife*. The geniuses are there again, doing their work, offering their offerings. This time, I look also at the audience, at the people around me. A full bright moon peers over the trees. I look at the silver-haired woman next to me. At the bearded man a few feet away. At another man nearby, who is wearing a yarmulke. At an Asian child, sleeping in her mother's lap. At the dark silhouettes of the people in front of me. They are each attended by a hovering genius. Some geniuses are pouring from their cornucopias, some seem to be resting. There are pixies in the air.

My own genius seems tired and self-satisfied. A busy and productive night.

Sing, sing, sing, sing . . .

Resources

To my knowledge, this is the only book specifically created to help you discover your genius. There are, however, many other books available concerning concepts such as commitment and personal mission. Here are a few of my favorites:

Lawrence Boldt has written an extraordinarily comprehensive career guide titled *Zen and the Art of Making a Living* (New York: Penguin, 1993). The second section of the book, "The Quest for Life's Work," will be particularly useful to those seeking their own mission.

Stephen Covey's work, especially *The Seven Habits of Highly Effective People* (New York: Fireside, 1989), is also very comprehensive and practical. It will be particularly useful to those who have detected their mission and are asking, "Now what?"

Phillip Berman has edited the writing of thirty-two well-known men and women about how they have put their beliefs into action in a book titled *The Courage of Conviction* (New York: Dodd, Mead and Company, 1985).

The list of contributors includes Joan Baez, Mario Cuomo, the Dalai Lama, Norman Cousins, and Benjamin Spock—quite an eclectic mix. The book offers suggestions from these people as well as inspiring stories.

David Kiersey and Marilyn Bates's book, *Please Understand Me* (Del Mar, CA: Prometheus Nemesis, 1984), presents a test that enables readers to determine their personality type. The test is based on the more comprehensive and well-researched Myers-Briggs Type Indicator. Many people who attend workshops like those described in this book have found clues to their genius within the description of their personality type in both *Please Understand Me* and the data provided by the Myers-Briggs Indicator.

My own *Artful Work: Awakening Joy, Meaning, and Commitment in the Workplace* (San Francisco: Berrett-Koehler, 1995) is, of course, also one of my favorites. It applies the assumptions of artists about their work to all work.

Richard Leider and David Shapiro wrote *Repacking Your Bags* (San Francisco: Berrett-Koehler, 1994) for people who want to lead a full life. Their perspective on purpose is useful and refreshing, and their ideas about ''lightening your load'' have made a profound difference for me.

Julia Cameron's *The Artist's Way* (New York: Putnam Berkley, 1992) is a miracle of a book. Although it was written for aspiring and working artists, Cameron's perspective that creative expression is the natural direction of life makes this an empowering book for anyone who is willing to take time for it.

Peter Koestenbaum's work as a clinical philosopher has touched me and helped me think more deeply about my own work. The most comprehensive compendium of Peter's exceptional thinking is in his book, *The Heart of Business* (San Francisco: Saybrook, 1987).

The search for your genius and mission is also an exploration of the terrain that lies beneath the surface of life. Many writers have aided my exploration of that terrain. Among them are James Hillman (*The Soul's Code*), Sam Keen (*Hymns to an Unknown God* and *Fire In the Belly*), Marianne Williamson (*A Return to Love*), Robert Bly (*Iron John*, as well as many books of poetry), Gary Zukav (*The Seat of the Soul)*, Stephen Nachmano-vitch (*Free Play*), David Whyte (*The Heart Aroused)*, Lyall Watson (*Life-tide*), Deepak Chopra (especially *The Seven Spiritual Laws of Success)*, and Thomas Moore (*Care of the Soul)*. And, of course, Victor Frankl (*Man's Search for Meaning*).

Notes and References

Chapter 1: Your Genius

"The forms of things are derived from their genius": William Blake, *The Portable Blake* (Alfred Kazin, editor) (New York: Viking Penguin, 1946), p. 79.

Jane Hissey, *Old Bear* (New York: Philomel Books, 1986).

Stephen Covey, *The Seven Habits of Highly Effective People* (New York: Fireside, 1989).

James Redfield, *The Celestine Prophecy* (New York: Warner, 1993).

Deepak Chopra, *The Seven Spiritual Laws of Success* (San Rafael, CA: Amber-Allen, 1994).

"You have a talent that is unique": Deepak Chopra, *The Seven Spiritual Laws of Success* (San Rafael, CA: Amber-Allen, 1994), p. 98.

"An inspection of his chair . . .": Sir Arthur Conan Doyle, *The Adventures of Sherlock Holmes* (New York: A Tor Book, 1989), p. 167.

"The key rattled in the lock": Sue Grafton, *B is for Burglar* (New York: Bantam, 1985), p. 205.

Chapter 2: Noticing

"How can I be useful . . .": Vincent Van Gogh in Laurence Boldt, *Zen and the Art of Making a Living* (New York: Penguin, 1993), p. 95.

"I could think about these hopelessly complicated problems undisturbed": Werner Heisenberg, *Physics and Beyond: Encounters and Conversations* (New York: Harper Torchbooks, 1972), p. 77.

"I was immediately convinced": Werner Heisenberg, *Physics and Beyond: Encounters and Conversations* (New York: Harper Torchbooks, 1972), p. 77.

"If I continue to take in data": These lines are sometimes called "The Gestalt Prayer," and I first heard them from Jonno Hanafin, who is affiliated with the Gestalt Institute of Cleveland. Neither Jonno nor others that I spoke to at the Institute know the source. Appparently, the author is anonymous.

"Established the much needed bridge": Werner Heisenberg, *Physics and Beyond: Encounters and Conversations* (New York: Harper Torchbooks, 1972), p. 78.

Chapter 3: What Is Genius?

"All men have a genius": Ananda Coomeraswamy, *Christian and Oriental Philosophy of Art* (New York: Dover, 1956), p. 38.

"The law of Dharma says that every human being has a unique talent": Deepak Chopra, *The Seven Spiritual Laws of Success* (San Rafael, CA: Amber-Allen, 1994), p. 98.

"No man . . . can be a genius": Ananda Coomeraswamy, *Christian and Oriental Philosophy of Art* (New York: Dover, 1956), p. 38.

Dictionary definitions of genius are from *The Random House College Dictionary*, 1975.

Descriptions of the genius of Classical Rome are from various sources, including Pierre Grimal, *The Concise Dictionary of Classical Mythology* (Cambridge, MA: Blackwell, 1990), p. 160.

"And she sent with each": Plato, *Phaedo* (Perseus Project, Tufts University: <http://medusa.perseus.tufts.edu/cgi->, <bin/text?lookup+plat.+rep.+620e&word=genius>)

"And so it is said": Plato, *Phaedo* (Perseus Project, Tufts University: <http://medusa.perseus.tufts.edu/cgi->, <bin/text?lookup+plat.+phaedo+107d&word=genius>).

"You are born with a character" James Hillman, *The Soul's Code* (New York: Random House, 1996), p. 7.

The references to Socrates were adapted from Clarke University Philosophy Department (<http://www.clarke.edu/departments/philosophy/apology/aplg0237.htm>)

"At birth the two of you": Robert Bly, *The Sibling Society* (Reading, MA: Addison-Wesley, 1996), p. 211.

"I find more and more that my style": William Blake, *The Portable Blake* (Alfred Kazin, editor) (New York: Viking Penguin, 1946), p. 176.

"It is a positive purposeful force": Gary Zukav, *The Seat of the Soul* (New York: Fireside, 1990), p. 31.

"Each person bears a uniqueness": James Hillman, *The Soul's Code* (New York: Random House, 1996), p. 6.

Chapter 4: Frustration and Curses

"Your self-expression is your gift to the world": Laurence Boldt, *Zen and the Art of Making a Living* (New York: Penguin, 1993), p. 9.

"Utterly exhausted and rather tense": Werner Heisenberg, *Physics and Beyond: Encounters and Conversations* (New York: Harper Torchbooks, 1972), p. 77.

"Blocking the fulfillment of man's natural drives": Hans Selye, *Stress without Distress* (New York: Signet, 1974), p. 76.

Chapter 5: Telling Stories

"There is no off position on the genius switch": David Letterman (quoted in <http://www.westnet.com/~chris/weird/1995/april/0048.html>).

Chapter 6: Solving the Puzzle

"The orderly and wise soul": Plato, *Phaedo* (Perseus Project, Tufts University: <http://medusa.perseus.tufts.edu/cgi->,   <bin/text?lookup +plat.+phaedo+108b&word+genius>).

"A felt sense is not a mental experience": Eugene Gendlin, *Focusing* (New York: Bantam, 1982), p. 32.

Chapter 7: Searching Together

"Each soul brings the particular configuration": Gary Zukav, *The Seat of the Soul* (New York: Fireside, 1990), p. 234.

Chapter 8: Commitment to a Mission

"Being human is directed to something": Victor Frankl, *The Will to Meaning* (New York: Meridian, 1988), p. 50.

"Beautiful airy rooms": Mikiel Azzopardi, "A Story of Something Beautiful." The story was sent to me by Monsignor Azzopardi's friend, Lewis Portelli.

"Perhaps one of his greatest achievements": Lewis Portelli, "Mgr. Micheal Azzopardi: An Appreciation by Lewis Portelli," *The Sunday Times* (Malta), May 31, 1987.

"Always looking ahead and beyond": Lewis Portelli, "Mgr. Micheal Azzopardi: An Appreciation by Lewis Portelli," *The Sunday Times* (Malta), May 31, 1987.

"Everyone has his own specific vocation": Victor Frankl, *Man's Search for Meaning* (New York: Touchstone, 1984), p. 113.

Chapter 9: Detecting Your Mission

"My business is circumference": *Selected Poems and Letters of Emily Dickinson*, Robert N. Linscott, editor (New York: Doubleday, 1959), p.25.

How we are best suited to serve humanity: Deepak Chopra, *The Seven Spiritual Laws of Success* (San Rafael, CA: Amber-Allen, 1994), p. 100.

"What is the message you want your life to proclaim": Laurence Boldt, *Zen and the Art of Making a Living* (New York: Penguin, 1993), p. 161.

"The mission only we can do": James Redfield, *The Celestine Prophecy* (New York: Warner, 1993), p. 141.

"A calling from a place": Thomas Moore, *Care of the Soul* (New York; HarperCollins, 1992), p. 181.

"A spiritual calling involves four elements": Sam Keen, *Hymns to an Unknown God* (New York: Bantam Books, 1994), p. 278.

"Vocation as a call": Matthew Fox, *The Reinvention of Work* (San Francisco, HarperSanFrancisco, 1994), p. 102.

"Purpose as cosmic role": Matthew Fox, *The Reinvention of Work* (San Francisco, HarperSanFrancisco, 1994), p. 106.

"We all have a spiritual purpose": James Redfield, *The Celestine Prophecy* (New York: Warner, 1993), p. 146.

"I think each of us has an internal monitor": Stephen Covey, *The Seven Habits of Highly Effective People* (New York: Fireside, 1989), p.128.

"One should not search": Victor Frankl, *Man's Search for Meaning* (New York: Simon & Schuster, 1984), p. 113.

"Discover your divinity": Deepak Chopra, *The Seven Spiritual Laws of Success* (San Rafael, CA: Amber-Allen, 1994), p. 101.

"We are to do what there is a deep": Marianne Williamson, *A Return to Love* (New York: HarperCollins, 1992), p. 192.

"It was as if a great bell called to me": Marion Zimmer Bradley, *The Mysts of Avalon* (Sphere Books, UK, 1984).

"We must never forget": Victor Frankl, *Man's Search for Meaning* (New York: Simon & Schuster, 1984), p. 116.

"We are not merely the phsyical creation": James Redfield, *The Celestine Prophecy* (New York: Warner, 1993), p. 138.

"If you view your life as one story": James Redfield, *The Celestine Prophecy* (New York: Warner, 1993), p. 139.

Chapter 10: Self-Responsibility and Support

"We can change ourselves": Rita Mae Brown in *The Courage of Conviction* (Phillip Berman, editor) (New York: Dodd, Meade & Company, 1985), p. 29.

"The existential ultimate concerns": Peter Koestenbaum, *The Heart of Business* (San Francisco: Saybrook, 1987), p. 72.

Epilogue

"She is pouring out a cornucopia": Stephen Nachmanovitch, *Free Play: The Power of Improvisation in Life and the Arts* (New York: Tarcher/Putnam, 1990), p. 36.

Blake's *Bright-Eyed Fancy* is reproduced in black-and-white in Stephen
  Nachmanovitch's *Free Play* (New York: Tarcher/Putnam, 1990), p. 38.
  A larger black-and-white print is in Irene Taylor's *Blake's Illustrations
  to the Poems of Gray* (Princeton: Princeton University Press, 1971).
The playbill for the Cincinnati Pops Orchestra's *1996 Concerts in the Park*
  credits Louis Prima as the composer of "Sing, Sing, Sing" for the motion picture *The Benny Goodman Story.*

Index